Spiritual Answers

— for —

Perilous Times

Spiritual Answers
— for —
Perilous Times

Answers About God and His Actions

Norma E. Sawyers

DOGWOOD PUBLISHING
BOLIVAR, MO 65613

Published by Dogwood Publishing, 116 West Buffalo, Bolivar,
MO 65613.

Printed in the United States of America

Publisher's Cataloging-in-Publication
(Provided by Quality Books, Inc.)

Sawyers, Norma E. (Norma Eileen), 1943-
    Spiritual answers for perilous times : answers about
God and his actions / by Norma E. Sawyers. -- 1st ed.
    p. cm.
    Includes bibliographical references.
    LCCN 2002090342
    ISBN 0-9630031-1-9

    1. Suffering--Religious aspects--Christianity.
    2. Terrorism--United States--Religions aspects. 3. God.
    I. Title.

BV4909.S39 2002   248.8'6
                    QBI02-701229

Contents

This know also,
that in the last days
perilous times
shall come.

—2 Tim 3:1

1

Real Questions

Have you ever had questions about God? Have you ever wondered who He was or what He was like or what He does? If you have, you're not alone—especially now—in wake of the September 11 terrorist attacks upon America and other recent terrifying events. Millions of hurting people in our country and around the world are desperately seeking answers to questions about God and His actions, such as: Why did God allow this atrocity to occur? Does He care about our suffering? Is God really "there"? How do I cope with death?

The issue of coping with death is no academic question with me. On an overcast day in March of 1982, something terrible happened and my little world exploded. I remember the day all too well: gray skies threatening snow flakes, ambulance attendants administering CPR at a motorcycle/truck accident scene, the comatose body of my fifteen-year-old daughter Karen slowly giving up life. Even now, twenty years later, it is painful for me to recall events leading to her death two days later from brain injuries suffered in that horrible crash.

Forgive me, but I can't write about the details of my daughter's death, for I can't subject myself to that again. But I can tell you something about her as a person; details about her brief life are forever etched in my memory. I can almost see Karen now. Most days after school, she would come bounding into my beauty salon business, blonde hair swinging, eager to share with me some tidbit about her day. "Hi, mom," she would cheerfully greet me as she held out her arms to give me a hug. "Guess what happened today?", she might add before proceeding to fill me in on some important aspect of her day. Of course, there were also times when things didn't go well at school, when the lilt was missing from her walk and the joy was absent from her greeting. Life is like that for teenagers, and Karen's life was no exception. The majority of the time though, my popular girl was happy, engrossed in her school work, her extracurricular activities such as sports and cheer leading, and her busy social life. That was my daughter Karen, the special person I will miss all my days on this earth.

And I can also tell you something about how her death affected my life. It led me to question God, to look for answers. In the days following Karen's death, a number of burning questions seared my soul like hot coals, such as: Why did God take my daughter? If God is loving and capable of miracles, why didn't He intervene in my situation? Does it make me a bad person to be angry with God because He did not?

Those were not simple, easy questions, but profound, real questions that plagued my soul night and day. And those questions led to even more questions, to an all out search for answers about my Creator. But God met me in that search, restoring my soul, healing my pain, answering my questions. Yet something else happened too. As a result of my own ordeal, I gained a real empathy for other people facing real life questions about God and His actions. That is why I'm writing this book.

Most folks question God at one time or another. However, because of certain events in recent years men and women from countries around the world have concurrently questioned God. Why? The first event occurred on Wednesday, April 19, 1995, when something incomprehensible happened: a terrorist bomb lit the morning sky with a red-orange fireball, dissolving the north side of the Alfred P. Murrah Federal Building in downtown Oklahoma City, killing one hundred sixty nine people and injuring numerous others.

I will never forget the day of the bombing of the Murrah Federal building. Recently divorced from my husband of nearly 30 years, plagued to distraction with thoughts about events surrounding the ugly breakup, I struggled daily to keep myself sane. Alone with my housework and the heaviness of my thoughts, I decided to take a break and flipped on the television. Watching breaking news about the horrendous event unfolding before my eyes, I became transfixed to the tube, reduced to tears, devastated that such a catastrophe had happened.

To the people of the world, the outrage of Oklahoma City was summed up in a single image, at once both terrible and tender. On front pages worldwide, the photograph of one-year-old Baylee Almon—her mortally injured body covered in dust and insulation and blood, cradled tenderly in the arms of fire fighter Chris Fields—became the symbol of the horror and pain of Oklahoma City.

"Why the Children?", read a headline in the May 1, 1995, *Newsweek*. The article continues, "The random and senseless destruction of a government building shows a nation how vulnerable it is; the random destruction of innocent children shows how deep the pain can go."[1] The most chilling fact about the Oklahoma City bombing was that it struck not only adults but also these tiny children eating breakfast and playing in the

America's Kids day-care center on the second floor of the Murrah Federal Building.

The second series of events began on September 11, 2001, when a hijacked airliner became a missile of death as it slammed into a World Trade Center tower in lower Manhattan. The sickening horror of the first assault only grew as many of us watched another plane rip into the second World Trade Center tower. Shortly thereafter, the Pentagon, headquarters of America's national defense, was hit in this series of senseless strikes which claimed around 4,000 lives. Another hijacked airliner, United Airlines flight 93, crashed near Pittsburgh due to the heroic actions of passengers who intentionally confronted the terrorist hijackers, precipitating a crash in an open field, undoubtedly preventing hijackers from completing their nefarious intent to likewise crash that airliner, this time most probably into the White House or the United States Capitol building.

Turning on CNN that terrible day, hearing and seeing the dreadful news of what had occurred, I was totally stunned. I asked myself, *What is this? Reporters are saying America has been attacked. How can this be?* Trying to comprehend the happenings, I was incredulous. I wondered: *How could anyone be so cruel, so monstrous as to use passenger airliners, filled with live human beings, as weapons of destruction against thousands of other innocent people.* It all seemed surreal, like a nightmare from which I longed to open sleepy eyes, and say: "It was just a horrible dream!" But what I saw was not a dream. Planes did pierce towers, and buildings did collapse. It was real! Along with millions of other people around the world, I cried.

Do you remember where you were when you first learned on September 11 that America had been attacked? On that day, the wrenching sight of passenger planes deliberately flown into symbols of America's economic and military strength became sharply engraved into the collective memory not only of the people of America, but also of the people of the world. America became a different nation that day, for we had been attacked in a way without precedent, in evil intent and in malicious magnitude. Decades earlier, architect Minoru Yamasaki said: "The World Trade Center should, because of its importance, become a living representation of man's belief in humanity." In the end, though, the scarred skyline became a symbol of man's malice.

If tragedies of this magnitude could happen in America, to the lone superpower thought to be capable of protecting the world, then the most basic assumptions of men and women worldwide—for security, for rationality, for decency—seemed tenuous indeed. Is it any wonder that in country after country, millions upon millions of human beings questioned, "What is this world coming to?"

Man's inhumanity to man has always evoked questions about God. Questions of this nature tortured Elie Wiesel. His graphic book, *Night*, describes scenes and tragedies from the holocaust of World War II that will pierce your heart like a dagger. This teenage Jew saw atrocities no young person should ever view— babies pitchforked, entire families shoved into a furnace exuding the stench of burning human flesh, little tots hanged. Francois Mauriac, in writing the foreword to Wiesel's book, describes the impact of one of those events: "On that day, horrible even among those days of horror, when the child watched the hanging (yes) of another child, who, he tells us, had the face of a sad angel, he heard someone behind him groan: 'Where is God? Where is He? Where can He be now?'"[2]

So many of you have questioned God. You've suffered your own personal heartaches—hurts, disappointments, losses—that caused real questions in your mind. Perhaps you've experienced the raw, unrelenting pain accompanying arthritis or some other crippling affliction. Perhaps you've witnessed the disastrous results of an accident caused by a drunken driver, leaving a young woman dead and her small children motherless. Perhaps you've watched as a loved one slowly died of cancer or as a friend was subjected to the ravages of another dread disease.

Suffering comes in a thousand shapes and sizes and goes by a variety of different names: sickness, fear, disappointment, loneliness, ridicule, rejection, death. It results from war, famine, crime, natural disasters, and, as we've so recently experienced, man's inhumanity to man. And it causes you to wonder why God allows all of the pain.

Deeply, deeply troubled by the profound questions of life, we wonder: Who is God? What kind of God is He? Does He really care? Yet so many times we are reluctant to voice the awesome questions lurking just beneath the surface. Somehow we have been made to feel that asking questions about God is wrong or sacrilegious. I remember as a young girl, long before I became a Christian, asking such a question in a Bible class. My teacher let me know right away that questions of that nature would not be tolerated. I really don't know for sure why my teacher reacted the way he did some 40 years ago, except perhaps he regarded verbal expressions about the nature and the actions of God as unacceptable. Humiliated by his sharp rebuke, I slunk down in my seat, resolved never to ask a question of that kind again.

At some time in your life, you may have asked a difficult question about God and received the same reaction. Don't despair. I have some good news for you. God doesn't object when we question; He's too great for that; He can handle any question. Far from discouraging our probing, He encourages us in our quest, saying, "Come now, let us reason together," (Isa 1:18). How different is God's attitude on verbal questioning compared to my Bible teacher's attitude. Whereas my teacher took a hush-hush view on such questioning, God remains completely open to our every question. This is because God knows our questions occur because they are part of our human frailty, our human existence. He understands that people have been questioning for centuries. In fact, the Bible relates several instances of people who questioned.

For example, when Job's world tumbled in, he sought an answer. If anyone ever deserved to question, it was this aging patriarch. Once a wealthy man, "the greatest man among all the people of the East" (Job 1:3), he lost everything material: his animals, his servants, his children, his health, and his friends. Despairing of God's dealings, Job wailed: "I loathe my very life; therefore I will give free rein to my complaint and speak out in the bitterness of my soul. I will say to God: Do not condemn me, but tell me what charges you have against me" (Job 10:1-2).

Listen to the prophet Jeremiah questioning God about the constant political, moral, and religious decline occurring in Judah during the time of his ministry: "You are always righteous, O Lord, when I bring a case before you. Yet I would speak with you about your justice: Why does the way of the wicked prosper? Why do all the faithless live at ease? (Jer 12:1).

13

Notice how Habakkuk complained of unchecked violence in Judah: Why do you make me look at injustice? Why do you tolerate wrong? Destruction and violence are before me; there is strife and conflict abounds. Therefore, the law is paralyzed, and justice never prevails" (Hab 1:3-4).

That sounds pretty contemporary, doesn't it? Conditions in the world really haven't changed very much. Job and Jeremiah and Habakkuk questioned thousands of years ago about some of the same issues that trouble us today. That helps me. I know it helps you also to see that present day folks aren't that different. When we ask why, we're not alone.

In fact, according to a recent article based on poll results in *Newsweek*: "Millions of Americans are embarking on a search for the sacred in their lives....No matter what path they take, the seekers are united by a sincere desire to find answers to profound questions, to understand their place in the cosmos."[3] Did you notice the article didn't say hundreds nor thousands, but millions of Americans are confronted with genuine difficulties and doubts? That's a lot of people! One or more of them could be someone you or I know: a relative, a friend, a neighbor, a co-worker, an acquaintance whose faith is blocked by troubling questions about God.

Think of the woman who just moved in down the street, whose husband recently deserted her. She's alone now with several children to clothe and feed and shelter. And she doesn't know where to turn. Think of the lady at work who has suffered from physical violence at the hands of her husband. Or the young girl who has been a victim of incest. We all know someone like that. These are real people, part of the millions who are searching for spiritual answers, who are in desperate need of God.

I want to invite you now to join me in my journey of personal discovery. For some time I have been searching for real answers for real questions about God, for answers that would satisfy both the heart and the mind. The answers aren't new. They are the same answers that have enlightened Christians down through the centuries. The answers aren't perfect. But perhaps they will create a spark in your mind that will result in further research and study. The answers are heartfelt though, the result of tragedy and heartbreak in my own life. And I want to share them with you.

Where do we begin? Each chapter of this book will address a specific question about the nature of God. These chapters will explore what the Bible teaches about Him: Who He is; What He is like; What He does.

However, our search for answers to questions about the nature of God must be preceded with answers to questions about His existence, for events such as the recent terrorist attacks might cause some folks to question whether God really exists. So we will look first in chapter 2 at evidence for God, at some objective arguments and the historical case supporting His existence. Then in later chapters we can look at some evidence about God, at the revelation of His character, nature, and attributes as set forth in Scripture, that gives us unassailable reasons to trust in Him.

I have written this book especially for those people who have questions about God and how He acts. If, in the wake of the sudden tragic changes in our world, you have been personally questioning God's role, I invite you to join me as we explore issues of vital importance to you. Who knows, you may find that you are not only getting answers for yourself, but also for a relative, a friend, or a neighbor struggling with the same issues.

2

How Can We Know There Is a God?

What does the beauty of a star-filled sky say to you? Does it say that there is a God? Or does it say nothing? What does it say to the widow of a fire fighter killed in the terrorist attacks of September 11, as she tries to walk off her sadness and grief under a silent late evening sky? What does it say to the young Manhattan restaurant worker, father of several small children, who has just been laid off from his job due to lack of business in the aftermath of the terrorism? What does it say to the New York City high school student who witnessed the horrifying scene of men and women jumping to their deaths from the World Trade Center towers on September 11? What about the scientist torn between the view that empirical science is the only source of knowledge and a conscience that tells her to believe what her senses can't see?

Is God there behind the expanse of the universe, behind the heroic deeds of fire fighters and policemen, behind the smile of a little baby? Is God there, in spite of acts of bioterrorism and the hatred of evil men? Is He there and can He be seen when the grieving, the abused, the misunderstood, and the lonely shed tears?

Have you ever noticed that our basic human questions can come in so many different forms? Perhaps you have heard someone ask a question such as one of the following: If God exists, why didn't he protect us on September 11, 2001? Why did He allow evil that brought so much destruction and loss? If God is in control, why are there so many natural disasters such as floods, earthquakes, and hurricanes? Why would a good God allow my loved one to die at a young age? When I look at the suffering that mankind endures, how can I believe that a God would not intervene to prevent all the pain? These questions reflect the tension that exists between the beauty of a clear night sky and the earth below that is all too often the scene of heartache and tragedy.

You and I can understand that doubts about God's existence might arise in the minds of some people. They wonder about an invisible God who refuses to appear in person to resolve all the questions about His existence and His dealings with mankind. For these and other reasons, honest skeptics need real, believable answers if they are to seriously consider the question of God's existence. They need to realize that those who believe in God do so as a result of sound reason and judgement.

But how can we know that God exists? According to the Bible, our source of truth, God has left us with a tremendous amount of data on which to base judgement about His existence. Both the Old and the New Testament clearly describe a number of converging lines of evidence that point to the existence of a personal God who, because of His eternal nature, is still present with us. These lines of evidence for belief in a personal God include: (1) evidence from Creation; (2) evidence from design; (3) evidence from history; and (4) evidence from Christ. So let's take a look now at the Bible's four-

pronged approach to letting us know for sure that there
is a God.

EVIDENCE FROM CREATION

First, God is revealed through Creation. No one
can deny that our complex universe is a dazzling, majes-
tic marvel. Our heads spin at the mere contemplation of
its astounding vastness and grandeur. George Carey,
Archbishop of Canterbury, comments: "How can we
possibly absorb the fact that, as far as we can tell, the
universe consists of innumerable galaxies like our own;
the nearest one to us being 900,000 light years away!"[1]
I don't know about you, but I think that is amazing!

The question arises: How did the universe begin?
That is a natural question to ask, isn't it? Our minds are
so constituted as to expect that every effect must have a
cause. As Michael Green asserts, it will not do to assign
the whole thing to chance: "If the world is due to
chance, how is it that cause and effect are built into that
world at every turn? It isn't very rational to suppose that
chance gives birth to cause and effect! And it isn't very
rational to argue that the world which is based on cause
and effect is itself uncaused."[2]

In the universe around us we perceive a great
variety of effects produced by some cause adequate to
produce them. Whether looking through a telescope at
the constellations of stars, listening to the crashing roar
of a waterfall, catching our breath at the sight of a
tremendous mountain range, marveling at the glory of a
sunrise or the beauty of a fragile flower or the awesome-
ness of a storm at sea, we must say with humility: God
created these things. Something deep inside causes us to
conclude that the cause of the universe is God, a being

possessed of sufficient power and intelligence to contrive and bring about marvelous effects such as these!

At this point some of you may be asking, "But who made God?" That's a tough question, isn't it? However, reason tells us that although we can keep going back from cause to effect, we cannot keep going back forever without admitting a Being who has existed forever. That Forever Being is God, who, as Ernest S. Williams explains, "alone is eternal, self-existent, and independent, the only Uncaused. This is an overwhelming thought. It is, however a true thought, for He who caused all things had to be before all things. Therefore He alone is Uncaused,…the One possessing all power, the source of all that is."[3] There could never have been a first effect if there had not been a First Cause, "God …the builder of everything" (Heb 3:4).

So in contemplating the immensity and variety of nature, we are constrained to believe in a Creator. Indeed, the Bible asserts that the universe is a testimony to God's existence, that the eloquent voice of God can be heard throughout creation: "The heavens declare the glory of God; the skies proclaim the work of His hands. Day after day they pour forth speech; night after night they display knowledge" (Ps 19:1-2).

EVIDENCE FROM DESIGN

A second way God is revealed is through design. When we look at the universe we realize it looks like it was planned by a great Designer. Whether we are looking at nature through a telescope, a microscope, or with our unaided vision, the facts reveal amazing order and mathematical design!

Gazing through a telescope, we see the intricate pattern of the movement of bodies in the universe, including pinpoint timing in their courses in relation to each other. We observe that the earth, in regard to its exact distance from the sun and its accurate journey through our solar system, possesses the necessary prerequisites for the temperate climate we enjoy. Elaborating on the seeming design of our earthly habitation, which whirls through space and turns on its axis at one thousand miles per hour, Dallas M. Roark says: "A speed of one hundred miles per hour would make the nights too long and the days too hot so that the earth would alternately freeze and burn. The earth's proximity to the sun is such that it is at the right distance to secure enough heat but not overheat....In many ways, the earth appears to be designed for life."[4]

Peering into a microscope at snowflakes, we discover that no two are alike. William T. Bently, an expert in photomicrography (photographing what is seen through a microscope), who worked for over a third of a century photographing snow crystals, observed three outstanding facts: "First, that no two were alike; second, that each was a beautiful pattern; third, that invariably each was six-pointed."[5] Isn't that remarkable? In the presence of such evidence of design, multiplied by countless variations, how can we doubt the existence and handiwork of an omnipotent Designer?

We also see complexity implying an intelligent Designer in the formation of various parts of the body, and especially of the eye. Have you ever really thought about your eyes? Evidence of design is obviously involved in their structure for sight, in their ability for motion, in their instinct against harm, and in their apparatus for self-preservation. The delicate intricacy of the eye and the interrelatedness of its parts attest to a Designer, to a Creator who knew what He was doing.

These are only a few illustrations of the presence of design and order within the universe. As we observe this order and design in the world and in the universe around us, we conclude it to be the product of a Master Designer, of God, "the Creator of the ends of the earth" (Isa 40:28).

EVIDENCE FROM HISTORY

A third way God is revealed is through the evidence of history. The uniqueness of the Christian message lies in its claim to be real historical truth. Christianity declares that around 2,000 years ago, Jesus Christ lived, taught, and died on earth in a small area of the Middle East, mostly in what is now Israel. That is not just a myth or fable, but a confirmed fact of history! The historic nature of the Christian faith distinguishes it from all other religions. In other religions the historical element takes a secondary place to the teachings. For instance, in Buddhism, the historical Buddha is irrelevant except as the source of his teachings. In contrast, the Christian tradition rests on historical facts about events. For example, the teachings on the atoning death of Jesus Christ would be nonsense unless Jesus had really died on the cross in history.

Because Christianity rests on a historic foundation, we have a means of verifying its truth. Clark H. Pinnock observes that through research and analysis we can check out the truth claims of the gospel historically: "The gospel makes a claim, and the claim can be tested by anyone who takes the trouble....The beauty of the gospel consists in its openness to examination. God has revealed Himself in time-space history (Jn 1:14). Christ was a public figure, and His resurrection a public event....God acted in history, and it is in history that we seek Him."[6]

What evidence is there to prove that the historical facts about Jesus Christ are really true? Examining the historical records, we note that the facts about Christ's life, teachings, and death are attested by strong proofs that declare them to be true. You may be surprised to learn, as I was, that these facts are acknowledged not only in historical writings from Christian sources, but also from Jewish and Gentile writings. Although most of these writings are secondary sources, not firsthand knowledge of the events of the life of Christ, they are valuable because they testify to Jesus' existence and confirm the basic record of His life as recorded in the New Testament. Check Appendix A for a listing of some of the best sources.

Godfrey Robinson and Stephen Winward note that enough material exists from early Jewish and Gentile non-Christian sources to compile a brief summary of the life and work of Jesus, as follows: "Jesus did in fact live; He taught and gathered disciples around Him, and was known for His wonderful acts or miracles. He was executed by crucifixion under the procurator Pontius Pilate, but the faith which He founded continued and grew stronger after His death. His followers, called Christians, worshipped Him as God, and this worship led to strife with both Jews and Gentiles. Such are seven distinct points which can be ascertained apart altogether from the witness of the New Testament."[7]

Since this summary agrees in detail with the biblical records, we are furnished with outside corroboration of the eye-witness accounts by the New Testament writers. Therefore, the historical nature of the life of Jesus is not an issue. Twenty-seven different New Testament documents written by people living in the first century who

23

had personal contact with Jesus testify to the facts about His life. The Christ in whom they believed is a definite person, of whose life and deeds and sayings a record has been preserved. We are able to add to their testimony that of the Jewish and Gentile sources.

Concerning the facts about Jesus, modern historical research leaves no room for reasonable doubt. As historian J. Gilchrist Lawson so aptly said: "The legendary, or mythical, theory of Christ's existence is not held by any one worthy of the name scholar. The historical evidences of Christ's existence are so much greater than those in support of any other event in ancient history; no candid scholar could reject them without also renouncing his belief in every event recorded in ancient history."[8]

It is clearly evident that Jesus Christ was a real figure of history, that He "became flesh and made his dwelling among us. [And] we have seen His glory" (John 1:14).

EVIDENCE FROM CHRIST

The fourth and ultimate way God has revealed himself to mankind is through Jesus Christ. The Christian religion stands or falls with the person of Christ, for Christianity is based on the belief that Jesus is Deity, "the true God and eternal life" (1 John 5:20).

History shows us that Jesus really lived, but how do we know that He is the true God? Scripture notes that the decisive proof is the resurrection of Jesus Christ, because God has "given proof of this to all men by raising Him from the dead" (Acts 17:31). Jesus' resurrection undeniably confirms His claim to be God's Son. As Paul wrote, Jesus "was declared with power to be the Son of God by His resurrection from the dead"

(Rom 1:4). Because of the resurrection, we know that Jesus was indeed the Messiah, the Lord, and the Son of God.

In considering the resurrection, there are two basic questions for us to ask: Is it certain that Jesus really died? And is it certain that He actually rose from the grave?

WAS JESUS REALLY DEAD?

Some people have suggested that Jesus wasn't really dead after the crucifixion but merely fainted and later revived in the cool of the rock tomb? Could that be what happened?

There are four reasons why this suggestion couldn't be the case. Consider the following background material. The crucifixion took place on the day before an important Jewish Sabbath, so it was important to the Jews that the bodies of Jesus and the two criminals executed with Him not remain on public display as this would defile the Sabbath. Therefore, the Jewish authorities asked that all three be released from their sufferings before dusk, the Judean procurator Pontius Pilate gave authorization, and the execution soldiers proceeded to hasten the death of the two criminals. However, the account goes on to record that when the soldiers came to Jesus, they "found that He was already dead" (John 19:33). Nevertheless, "one of the soldiers pierced Jesus' side with a spear" (John 19:34).

First, we know Jesus was really dead because the execution soldiers, who were certainly familiar with the evidence of death following crucifixion, saw that He was dead. Second, the Roman authorities knew Jesus was dead. When Joseph of Arimathea asked for the body for burial, Pontius Pilate knew Jesus was dead, after he "learned from the centurion that it was so" (Mark 15:45). Third, the Jewish authorities were satisfied that Jesus was dead because the next day, gathering with Pilate, they referred to a prophecy Jesus had made "while He was still alive" (Matt 27:63). Fourth, the Christians also undoubtedly believed that Jesus was dead. John, a beloved friend of Jesus, who actually saw one of the soldiers pierce the side of the Lord, stated that the act brought "a sudden flow of blood and water" (John 19:34).

Michael Green writes of John's observation: "We are told on eyewitness authority that 'blood and water' came out of the pierced side of Jesus (John 19:34,35). The eyewitness clearly attached great importance to this. Had Jesus been alive when the spear pierced His side, strong spouts of blood would have emerged with every heart beat. Instead, the observer noticed semi-solid dark red clot seeping out, distinct and separate from the accompanying watery serum. This is evidence of massive clotting of the blood in the main arteries, and is exceptionally strong medical proof of death. It is all the more impressive because the evangelist could not possibly have realized its significance to a pathologist. The 'blood and water' from the spear-thrust is proof positive that Jesus was already dead."[9]

Clearly Jesus was dead. It is inconceivable that the executioners, the Roman authorities, the Jewish authorities, and the Christian who witnessed the "blood and water" were all deceived.

DID JESUS REALLY ARISE?

This brings us to our second question: Did Jesus actually rise from the grave? One thing is certain—the tomb was definitely empty. Testimony by competent witnesses, both friends and enemies, certifies this fact. The women, the disciples, and the Roman guards all agreed the tomb was empty.

But how shall we account for the absence of the body of Jesus from the tomb? That the disciples hadn't stolen it is evident from the testimony of the soldiers who were bribed by the chief priests and the elders to tell the following story: "You are to say, 'His disciples came during the night and stole Him away while we were asleep.'" (Matt 28:13). Paul E. Little says of this theory concocted by the Jews: "They gave the soldiers money and told them to explain that the disciples had come at night and stolen the body while they were asleep. That story is so obviously false that Matthew doesn't even bother to refute it! What judge would listen to you if you said that while you were asleep your neighbor came into your house and stole your television set? Who knows what goes on while he's asleep? Testimony like this would be laughed out of any court."[10]

In addition, if the disciples stole the body, what explains their sudden change of character from timid, fearful, and panicky men to fearless proclaimers of the gospel? Before Easter, the disciples were clearly discouraged because of the crucifixion. However, by the day of Pentecost seven weeks later, they were boldly proclaiming the name of Jesus to the multitudes in Jerusalem. Also, all of the disciples endured great suffering because of their testimony about the risen Lord, most to the point of death. Is it at all reasonable to think that these men gave their lives to the cause of Christ if they had stolen the body and knew the resurrection was just a lie? Such behavior would have been inexplicable.

Concerning the profound change of character in these men, Little observes: "What was it that changed a band of frightened, cowardly disciples into men of courage and conviction? What was it that changed Peter from one who, the night before the Crucifixion, was so afraid for his own skin that he three times denied he even knew Jesus, into a roaring lion of the faith? Some 50 days later Peter risked his life by saying he had seen Jesus risen from the dead....Only the bodily resurrection of Christ could have produced this change."[11]

Likewise, it is evident that the body of Jesus had not been stolen by the authorities. Since the Jewish and Roman leaders were staunchly against the Christian movement, we may safely presume that, had they been able, they would have produced the body of Jesus to disprove the Christian claim that He had risen. Yet, when the disciples began proclaiming the risen Christ, the authorities were unable to produce the body to show the claim was untrue.

Josh McDowell notes that the Church "was founded on the resurrection, and disproving it would have destroyed the whole Christian movement. However, instead of any such disproof, throughout the first century, Christians were threatened, beaten, flogged and killed because of their faith. It would have been much simpler to have silenced them by producing Jesus' body, but this was never done."[12] John R.W. Stott adds that the silence of Christ's enemies "is as eloquent a proof of the resurrection as the apostles' witness."[13]

CHRIST IS RISEN!

We are left with only one reasonable explanation for the absence of the body of Jesus from the tomb: He arose from the grave! The resurrection of Jesus is one of the most well-documented events in the ancient world. As Pinnock points out: "There are very few events of ancient history better attested with sound evidence than the resurrection of Jesus Christ. It is as secure in its place in the annals of history as almost any other event."[14]

Christ is risen, indeed! The risen Christ has gone forth into the world, transforming human beings in every nation, tongue, and tribe of this earth. Countless millions of people can testify that Christ, alive from the dead, has entered into their lives and changed them. Christ is the One who says, "I am the Living One; and I was dead, and behold I am alive for ever and ever!...And whoever lives and believes in me will never die" (Rev 1:18; John 11:26).

In this chapter we have observed overwhelming evidence from Creation, from design, from history, and from Christ that point to the existence of God.

Returning to our earlier questions, what does the beauty of a star-filled sky say to the grieving fire fighter's widow, to the unemployed Manhattan restaurant worker, to the New York City student witnessing tragedy, to the scientist questioning the existence of a spiritual realm? It says there is a God. For He can be seen in the sky and all around them. He can be seen in the faces of New York City firemen and police officers as they carry on rescue efforts, in the faces of Americans crowded into blood-donation centers, eager to do something, anything to help those who endured the attack. He can be seen in the faces of little American kids donating one dollar to help suffering children in Afghanistan. He can be seen in acts of goodness and kindness and compassion everywhere, for truly, "love is from God" (1 John 4:7).

3

Is God a Real Person?

As America tries to recover and to regain some sense of normalcy after the terrorist attacks of September 11 and the subsequent anthrax bioterrorism attacks, as our people try to return to work and the "normal" affairs of life while the country wages a war on terrorism, a feeling of uneasiness continues to pervade our consciousness. If we were asked, many of us would have to admit that we are frightened. We may be frightened of flying, of being in tall buildings, of being in large crowds. We may even be frightened of opening our mail. We are trying to go on with life, to be brave. But under it all many of us are still a little nervous, a little scared.

In these times of apprehension, what we believe about God in regard to His personhood makes a big, big difference. The importance of discovering that God is personal cannot be emphasized enough to a generation that has often regarded God as the "force" which they hoped would "be with them." To some people, God is no more personal than a tree or a rock. They hope He exists, but they have no personal contact or relationship with Him.

If God were nothing more than a force, there would be little benefit for us in terms of personal relationship or involvement. A personal God, one who knows our needs and our fears and our feelings of vulnerability, is the kind of God who can help us most. Therefore, it is vitally important that we examine the concept that God is a real person.

But how is God like we are? Does He have a personality endowed with emotions as we have? Can we relate to Him in a personal way as we do with our friends? Do we share common characteristics such as a body? Can we see Him or experience Him through the five senses? The Bible says that mankind is made in God's own "image" and "likeness" (Gen 1:26-27). But what aspect of man is made in God's image?

The Bible explains that man has a dipartite nature—body and spirit, as Gen 2:7 explains: "The Lord God formed man of the dust of the ground, and breathed into his nostrils the breath of life; and *man became a living soul*" [KJV]. 1 Cor 15:45 concurs: "So it is written: 'The first *man* Adam *was made a living soul*'" [KJV]. Most Christian scholars believe that the eternal nature of man is to be a "living soul," that is a body plus spirit for eternity.

It is not man's physical body (which is subject to death), but his personality or spirit (which will never die) that was formed in God's image. When physical death occurs, the body is separated from the spirit: "The body without the spirit is dead" (Jas 2:26). So the personality or spirit of man is eternal, although the physical body will decay when physical death occurs.

Billy Graham stresses that personality does not require a physical body: "Here on earth we confine personality to the body. Our finite minds cannot envision personality that is not manifested through flesh and bones. We know that our own personalities will not always be clothed in the bodies they now inhabit. We know that at the moment of death our personalities will leave our bodies and go on to the destinations that await them. We know all this—yet it is difficult for us to accept it"[1]

A physical body is not a prerequisite for personality, but what exactly do we mean when we use such words as "person," or "personality"? How is God a person as we are? Six basic characteristics of personhood are: (1) life; (2) intelligence; (3) self-consciousness; (4) self-determination; (5) purpose; and (6) emotion.

LIFE

It should be obvious that the first requirement for personality is life. In reference to God's personality, Scripture speaks of "the living God" as opposed to an abstract principle or force. Its primary appeal is to what God does as a person in interaction with the people of His creation. Alan Richardson points out that the Hebrews "did not reach the notion of God as the Creator of the world as the final step of a long process of philosophical reasoning; they arrived at it as the result of their encounter with the living God in the sphere of history, in their dealings with Him as the controller of their national life and fortunes. It was from their experience of the activity of God in history that the Hebrew prophets learnt that God is personal, and it was from the Hebrew prophets that the world derived the conception of a personal God."[2] It is clear that a God who is revealed through His activity in history must be a living, personal God.

The personal nature of the God of the Bible sets Him apart from the gods of the East. In eastern thought, God is a part of nature: God is all and all is God. Thus

God is identified with nature and not held to be independent of or separate from it. But as Barry Seagren explains: "The Bible insists that this is not true. To God, not all things are the same. It is not true that everything is a part of God, not true that there is a bit of God in everything and everybody. Rather, He is a definite, distinct, discrete person."[3] God is not the universe but its Maker.

God as the Bible speaks of Him is overwhelmingly alive and active, the living God who sustains and orders all things by His word: "For the word of God is living and active. Sharper than any double-edged sword, it penetrates even to dividing soul and spirit, joints and marrow; it judges the thoughts and attitudes of the heart. Nothing in all creation is hidden from God's sight. Everything is uncovered and laid bare before the eyes of Him to whom we must give account" (Heb 4:12-13).

A living God is one to whom each of us must answer. Because He lives, He will judge even the thoughts and the attitudes of our hearts. Consequently, one reason many people find the idea of an impersonal God so attractive is that it gives them the comfort of believing in God without the unpleasant consequences. But our God is the living Lord, for He will come "to judge the earth. He will judge the world in righteousness and the peoples in his truth" (Ps 96:13).

INTELLIGENCE

The second characteristic of personality is intelligence. Human beings enjoy superior intellect, setting us apart from all other creatures. Human beings are endowed with minds inspired by incredible intelligence and creativity as exhibited in such areas as art and science and religion. Men and women ask questions, reason, and draw conclusions. We have the ability to learn from past experience and to respond to new challenges. We exhibit an abiding interest in our origins and purpose, wondering at our own existence. We have the ambition to elevate our lives, to reach out for something higher and greater than ourselves. We are deeply dissatisfied with mere mortality and the confines of our earthly habitation. And this is why we hunger and yearn for a deep relationship with God.

Thus we recognize that the human mind is controlled by more than the physical brain. Human thought transcends the brain as it reflects upon abstract concepts like wisdom, justice, and spirit. Of course, the human brain is being pulled into service when we think on such concepts, but it is not doing it alone.

George Carey relates that human mental processes go beyond mere organic electrochemical activity: "When we think of the powerful mind of Einstein, or the brilliance of Shakespeare, or the intuition, commitment, and scholarship of Madame Curie, we find ourselves rejecting the notion that all such activity is nothing more than an intricate network of nerve endings and pulsating electrical currents. No doubt such elements are included in the process but it is surely not enough to convey the reality of mind in our experience and life in general. No—what we might postulate is the strong possibility of a directive conscious intelligence, which is given to us as human beings and separates us from the rest of the animal kingdom."[4]

With whom do we share this mental faculty? This quality of life is something that links us to the heart of the universe, to God whose "understanding has no limit" (Ps 147:5). God is unlimited in knowledge; there is nothing that He does not know. God is all-knowing. In contrast, man's intelligence is limited. But the fact that man has intelligence—a mind to think, to reason, to plan—results from God's placing within man His own image. God is the source of intelligence, so man's ability to know, sense, and understand comes from Him.

SELF-CONSCIOUSNESS

A third mark of personality is self-consciousness. A person is the kind of being who can be self-aware of his or her own personhood. The fact that we know that we exist, that we are aware of our existence and personality, is evidence of our personhood.

Joseph F. Green states that man's value lies in the quality of his life called consciousness: "All of nature's size and beauty would mean nothing were it not for their recognition by some personal consciousness. There is no reason to believe that nature is aware of man; man, however, is aware of nature. In that awareness lies the appreciation of the values of the natural world....Nature without consciousness would be empty of all meaning and worth. Man alone in the natural world has enough consciousness to make meaning and worth possible."[5]

Self-consciousness is a quality God shares with people, which means that He is aware that He is God. One great statement in the Bible about the self-consciousness of God is contained in His words to Moses: "I AM WHO I AM" (Exod 3:14). Divine self-consciousness is also implied in 1 Cor 2:10 where the Spirit is described as searching "all things, even the deep things of God."

D.A. Carson emphasizes that God "is aware of His own existence, that He reasons, makes free decisions. He is an intelligent moral being, not merely an abstract idea, a 'thing' which somehow exercises fatalistic control over the universe, like a giant robot in a factory.

He acts and speaks because He consciously chooses to act and speak, deciding what He will do and what He will say."[6]
The fact that God is a self-conscious being capable of direct and significant communication with mankind, brings great comfort to our hearts. We can pray to a personal God, can believe that He knows and cares about what is going on in the world, for as Scripture tells us: "The earth is full of His unfailing love" (Ps 33:5).

SELF-DETERMINATION

Self-determination means freedom of choice in decision making. Freedom of choice and decision is a great gift from God, never unlimited, often misused, yet always present to distinguish mankind from all else in creation. Human beings are not mere biological organisms acting by reflex or instinct, but we are free within limits to rise above our circumstances and to direct our destinies through ideals and goals.

Mankind's capacity for goodness comes with this freedom of choice but also the alternative possibility for evil. Timothy McVeigh was motivated by evil when he bombed the Murrah Federal Building in Oklahoma City in April 1995. Likewise, the perpetrators of the September 2001 acts of terrorism upon America were driven by evil intent. God has given such people freedom of will, but rather than choosing to do good these individuals have freely chosen to do evil.

Many of us were unaware that five years before the terrorist attacks of September 11, Osama bin Laden declared war on the United States. The experts have told us that this illusive man was indeed the mastermind behind not only the September attacks, but also a number of other terrorist acts including the bombings of two of our embassies in East Africa several years ago. Bin Laden, the leader of the largest revolutionary Islamic group in the world, a man who inherited a fortune, used that money to carry out his evil design of a war against America. It is indeed tragic that men like McVeigh and bin Laden have chosen to misuse their freedom of choice for evil rather than good.

In contrast, the potential for much good can derive from self-determination—the possibility of seeking and discovering truth, of using our powers for fresh forms of creativity and for making the world around us better. And, most importantly, with our freedom of choice comes the capacity for loving, a choice that is far more than animal gregariousness or biological instinct. Because of this capacity, we are bidden to love God supremely and our neighbors as ourselves. It is mankind's capacity for goodness, for learning, and for loving that gives us a high dignity and provides meaning to the fact that we are made in God's likeness.

Self-determination is a definite hallmark of personality. God's choices are determined by Himself, just as are those of humans. With this freedom of personal choice, there is true personality.

PURPOSE

Human beings can react to the stimuli of future goals which have no real existence outside their own minds. This is what is meant by purpose, and it is another mark of personality. God has "eternal purpose" (Eph 3:11) which includes everything: "For from Him and through Him and to Him are all things" (Rom 11:36). Humans have purpose just as God does, but our purpose is limited by His purpose and plan. God's purpose includes everything, ours does not. His purpose is always fulfilled, ours does not always turn out as we planned. But His Lordship means there is purpose to all that is happening in our lives: "And we know that in all things God works for the good of those who love Him, who have been called according to His purpose" (Rom 8:28).

Though we may not be able to see or to understand His plan or His purpose, our Heavenly Father is on his throne and in control of our lives. Because Scripture says that God works for the good of those who love Him, we can feel encouraged despite the fact that life often presents us with difficult circumstances. We can know that the tortuous misfortunes of life do not have the last word, for the purpose of God for ultimate good in our lives will not be denied. If we truly love and believe in God, we have His promise that regardless of what tragedy befalls us, we will be with him forever. Thus, our Savior can turn even the greatest tragedy into the greatest good.

EMOTION

God is a person in the sense that He has emotions and feelings just as we do. Men and women can become emotional about events past or future. They can also have feelings without facts, creating emotion within the framework of their own minds. Thus feelings of hate and bitterness can exist when no real cause for them exists, as displayed by the extreme irrational hatred exhibited toward the United States by recent terrorists.

In fact, *radical* Muslims believe that Americans are the great Satan, that we are evil, and that we should be destroyed. Of course, it needs to be made clear that although bin Laden and his group are *extreme* followers of Islam, their viewpoint on the Islamic faith is not held by all Muslims. Many moderate Muslims are deeply grieved by what has happened, for they view Islam as a religion of peace.

Nevertheless, *radical* proponents of Islam believe in "jihad," the declaration of a "holy war." They give the Hadith, a record of Mohammed's life and sayings, higher authority than the Muslim holy book, the Koran. The Hadith records that when Mohammed was asked, "What is the best deed?"

He replied, "To believe in Allah and his apostle (Mohammed)."

The question was then asked, "What is the next (deed in goodness)?"

He replied, "To participate in jihad (religious war) in Allah's cause" [Sahih Bukhari Volume 1, Book 2, Number 25]. According to the Hadith, jihad is their second most important commandment.

Contrast the *extreme* viewpoint held by recent terrorists with the Christian view. Jesus was asked what is the greatest commandment. He answered, "'You shall love the Lord your God with all your heart, and with all your soul, and with all your mind.' This is the great and foremost commandment. The second is like it, 'You shall love your neighbor as yourself'" (Matt 22:37-39).

My friends, there is an infinite gulf between teachings espoused by Mohammed in the Sahih Bukhari and the teachings of Jesus Christ in the Bible that "you shall love your neighbor as yourself." So, beginning with His love, let's consider further the emotions of God.

LOVE

The Bible speaks over and over of God's great love in verses such as the following: "For God so loved the world that He gave His one and only son, that whoever believes in Him shall not perish but have eternal life" (John 3:16). "I have loved you with an everlasting love; I have drawn you with loving-kindness" (Jer 31:3). "But God demonstrates His own love for us in this: While we were still sinners, Christ died for us" (Rom 5:8). God's love, unlike ours, never fails. His forgiveness is remarkable, for when God forgives, it is despite the fact that He is the wounded party and has never sinned. In contrast, when we forgive, we remember that we, too, have sinned.

Though our ability to love is imperfect, its very presence is one of the characteristics of personality. So too, the perfect, unconditional love of our Christian God demonstrates that He is a real person.

ANGER

God can also show righteous anger! Scripture tells us that God feels wrath against all sin and all sinners: "The wrath of God is being revealed from heaven against all the godlessness and wickedness of men who suppress the truth by their wickedness" (Rom 1:18). John 3:36 says, "Whoever believes in the Son has eternal life, but whoever rejects the Son will not see life, for God's wrath remains on him." God's wrath is a necessary part of His justice. If God were indifferent to sin and to sinners, He would be denying His own holiness. This does not mean that God's anger is spiteful, arbitrary, or uncontrolled. But His anger occurs and is justified precisely because He is God, who rightly lays claim to our devotion and obedience.

Our anger all too often is the result of personal resentment arising from wounded pride or vanity, so it can be unjustified at times. But even when our anger is justified, we must exercise caution, for there is always danger that we may sin when we are angry. This is why God's Word tells us: "In your anger do not sin" (Eph 4:26). In and of itself, anger at sin and evil is not sinful. We must remember, however, that when we are angry at sin, we must still love the sinner.

Although we may sometimes sin in our anger, God gets angry but never sins. He will invariably be both loving and angry. His anger is an additional piece of evidence that He is a real person with emotions similar to ours.

SORROW

It is a mark of personality that we have sorrow and grief. But it is such a comfort to know that God feels sorrow as well, for He is a real person who understands our grief and sympathizes with our suffering as no other can.

Today, millions of Americans join together to share the grief and mourn the loss experienced by nearly 4,000 families who have had a loved one ripped from their grasp in the September 11 tragedy. Indeed, this is a calamity beyond our ability to express. But God knows about our sorrow, and He understands our pain, for Scripture informs us that the Messiah was "a man of sorrows, and familiar with suffering" (Isa 53:3). Scripture also tells us that "He heals the brokenhearted and binds up their wounds" (Ps 147:3).

That particular verse holds a deep meaning for me. Several years ago, during a time of extreme personal sorrow, I cried out to God for comfort. Opening the devotional book *Come Away, My Beloved* at random, I glanced down and read these words: "By my Spirit, I will mend the broken heart, I will pour warm, fragrant oil into the deep wound. For mine heart is fused with thy heart, and in thy grief, I am one with thee."[7] After reading the remainder of the brief but comforting devotional which seemed to speak directly to my needs, I closed the book and turned to my Bible. Also opening its pages at random, my glance fell on the words of Psalms 147:3: "He heals the brokenhearted and binds up their wounds."

Those words were a soothing balm for my raw wounds, a reminder that God was deeply concerned and cared for me. Tears streaming down my face, I thanked God for coming to me in my time of need.

Because God is personal, you and I have a friend who is able to "sympathize" with our weaknesses (Heb 4:15), who will "sustain" us if we simply cast our cares on Him: "Cast your cares on the Lord and He will sustain you" (Ps 55:22).

JOY

Personality is also characterized by the emotion of joy or happiness. God feels joy just as you and I do! Zephaniah 3:17 tells us: "The Lord your God is with you, He is mighty to save. He will take great delight in you, He will quiet you with His love, He will rejoice over you with singing." Isaiah 62:5 says: "As a bridegroom rejoices over his bride, so will your God rejoice over you." Nehemiah 8:10 relates that "the joy of the Lord is your strength."

When my little grandsons Neal, Hunter, and Landon were born, I felt great joy! And that joy continues! Every time I see my grandsons, or even think of them, the emotion of joy wells up in my heart.

Jesus also feels tremendous joy over every person who turns to Him for salvation and is born again: "I tell you, there is rejoicing in the presence of the angels of God over one sinner who repents" (Luke 15:10). Heaven is a place of rejoicing, and God is a person who possesses great joy for His people!

COMPASSION

Compassion is caring about people in need, and God has this emotion in abundance. For example, Psalm 103:13 says: "As a father has compassion on his children, so the Lord has compassion on those who fear Him." During his ministry here on earth, Jesus manifested compassion on many occasions. Matthew 9:36 relates: "When He saw the crowds, He had compassion on them, because they were harassed and helpless, like sheep without a shepherd." Matthew 15:32 adds: "Jesus called His disciples to Him and said, 'I have compassion for these people; they have already been with me three days and have nothing to eat. I do not want to send them away hungry, or they may collapse on the way.'"

The people of the United States have often exhibited compassion even toward their enemies. After past wars we have helped to rebuild the countries of those who fought against us, and during the recent war on terrorism in Afghanistan, we have shown compassion on innocent civilians in dire need by donating food and supplies.

The Bible speaks often of God's great mercies, graciousness, and compassion. How could we doubt that He is a real person after learning of his wonderful compassion?

Is God a real person? In this chapter we have explored six basic characteristics of personality that show us to be persons and God to be a person. Our Creator is a living, intelligent, self-conscious, self-determining, purposive, and emotional Being! He is a real person who loves us, who cares about us, and who is with us always in all circumstances.

Today Americans express fear of future evil that terrorists may inflict upon us. With the fall of the World Trade Center towers and the strike on the Pentagon, our traditional sources of strength and security seemed to topple. In less than seventy minutes, madmen armed with simple box cutters overwhelmed America's military might to deal strategic blows to the centers of our economic and military strength. Our false sources of strength had indeed failed us in our time of crisis. It is no wonder that the prospect of future terrorist attacks is enough to grab us by the neck and make us quake with fear.

But suddenly the realization dawns on us: Only God can protect our nation. We can search for the evil monsters responsible for the terrorism. We can round up, incarcerate, and perhaps execute those behind this outrage, but we know there are thousands of others in countries around the world ready and willing to take their place.

Evil has reared its venomous head against America, but God still retains ultimate control. Those who possess a personal relationship with Him need not live in a perpetual state of dread, because "God is our refuge and strength, an ever-present help in trouble. Therefore we will not fear,...Come and see the works of the Lord, the desolations he has brought on the earth. He makes wars to cease to the ends of the earth; He breaks the bow and shatters the spear, He burns the shields with fire. Be still and know that I am God; I will be exalted among the nations, I will be exalted in the earth. The Lord Almighty is with us; The God of Jacob is our fortress" (Ps 46:1,2,8-11).

Today the most important consideration for the people of America is that we draw closer to God as a nation, because we realize as never before that we are dependent upon him for strength and protection. When a nation stands sovereign under the protection of God, it is a sure truth that He will not fail them, for "blessed is the nation whose God is the Lord....The eyes of the Lord are on those who fear Him, on those who hope is in His unfailing love, to deliver them from death, and keep them alive in famine. We wait in hope for the Lord; He is our help and our shield. In Him our hearts rejoice, for we trust in His holy name. May your unfailing love rest upon us, even as we put our hope in you" (Ps 33:12,18-22).

4

Is There More Than One God?

The basic Christian teaching of the Trinity is included in the following: "There is one and only one living and true God. He is an intelligent, spiritual, and personal Being, the Creator, Redeemer, Preserver, and Ruler of the universe. God is infinite in holiness and all other perfections. To Him we owe the highest love, reverence, and obedience. The eternal God reveals Himself to us as Father, Son, and Holy Spirit, with distinct personal attributes, but without division of nature, essence, or being."[1] In short, the doctrine teaches that God is a unity, subsisting in three persons: the Father, the Son, and the Holy Spirit—all three of whom are one God. It is an old, old belief, which has held a depth of meaning for Christians all through the ages.

Why is it important for us to examine this doctrine? In this present time of crisis in our great nation, when the people of our country need so desperately to draw nearer to God, it is vital that this basic tenet of the Christian faith should be especially emphasized. False cults, sects, and religions exist that assign to our Lord and Savior Jesus Christ and to the Holy Spirit a nature and a position below that of true Deity. But the doctrine of the Trinity is essential to all facets of Christianity including redemption, revelation, fellowship, and prayer.

Concerning the work of redemption, all three members of the Godhead play critical roles in making our redemption from sin possible: the love of the Father prompted Him to send His Son into the world that we might live through Him; the love of Christ for sinners and His obedience to the will of His Father led Him to die as our substitute; and the loving ministry of the Holy Spirit applies the benefits of the blood of Christ to all who obtain God's free gift of eternal life.

Likewise, God's revelation of Himself to man is based on the nature of the Trinity. "As God can, in an absolute sense, communicate Himself inward in an act of self-revelation among the three Persons, so He is able, in a relative sense, to impart Himself outward in revelation and communication to His creation."[2]

Ultimate fellowship derives from the triune nature of God. Since God has perfect fellowship within His own being, absolutes for fellowship and love exist. And since God created us in His own image, we can have true fellowship with Him and with one another.

In addition, the way we approach God in prayer is dependent on the Trinity. In prayer the Holy Spirit intercedes for us, for we do not know what we ought to pray (Rom 8:26). And the Father is the One to whom we pray, but we must ask in the name of the Son (John 16:23-24).

For these and other reasons, the doctrine of the Trinity is of tremendous significance for men and women everywhere.

The Bible teaches the fact of the Trinity with the Old Testament foreshadowing, and the New Testament revealing the doctrine.

OLD TESTAMENT FORESHADOWING

Although the main evidence for the doctrine of the Trinity is found in the New Testament, we need to start with the Old. Since the New Testament is based on the Old, no statement of belief is complete unless it is seen in the context of the entire Bible. Like many Scripture teachings, the entire truth of the doctrine of the Trinity is not stated in the Old Testament, which provides *preparation* for redemption, while the New Testament presents *manifestation* of redemption. In particular the Old Testament contains undeveloped foreshadowings of the coming revelation of the Trinity.

During the some fifteen hundred years over which the Bible was written, God revealed Himself to man in a progressive way. He began by revealing that there is but one God, not three. One of the clearest and best known statements of God's unity is: "Hear, O Israel: The Lord our God, the Lord is one" (Deut 6:4). Isaiah 46:9 also declares: "Remember the former things, those of long ago; I am God, and there is no other; I am God, and there is none like me." Isaiah quotes God as saying: "Turn to me and be saved, all you ends of the earth; for I am God, and there is no other (Isa 45:22). Then again, Psalm 96:4-5 reiterates: "For great is the Lord and most worthy of praise; He is to be feared above all gods. For all the gods of the nations are idols."

These passages make it clear that there is only one God. "That God is one, and there is no other, that He has no equal, is the forceful testimony of above fifty passages of Scripture....No other truth of the Scripture, particularly of the Old Testament, receives more prominence than that of the unity of God."—Cerdo.

49

Our necessary conclusion then is that Deity is one God; one, and no more. Since there can be but one absolutely perfect, supreme and almighty Being, a multiplicity of gods would be a contradiction. Such a Being cannot be multiplied, nor pluralized. There can be but one ultimate, all-inclusive God.

Although there can be only one God, this does not exclude a plurality of persons in the Godhead, however. Therefore, in the Old Testament, God not only reveals His unity, but also begins revealing His diversity—His three-in-one nature—with important pointers foreshadowing the New Testament revelation of the Trinity. These pointers can be placed in three categories.

Plural Forms for God

Some passages use plural forms for God. For instance, one form of the name for God, *Elohim*, is plural. This is similar to the Hebrew word for *water* which is also in the plural since water can be thought of in terms of individual rain drops or in terms of the mass of water of the ocean. The plural form in this case points to "diversity in unity." Likewise, the same is true of the plural term *Elohim*.

There are also passages where God speaks of Himself in the plural. For example, when God said, "Let us make man in *our* image, in *our* likeness" (Gen 1:26), and "The man has now become like one of *us*" (Gen 3:22), plural forms were used. It is clear that God could not be talking to angels here, for angels cannot create nor help God create.

A plurality of persons is also expressed in Isaiah's vision: "Then I heard the voice of the Lord saying, 'Whom shall I send? And who will go for *us*?'" (Isa 6:8). This passage also indicates that within God Himself there is some kind of discussion or interchange of views.

A group of ideas in the Old Testament such as the *word of the Lord* and the *spirit of God* occur in connection with God's active dealing with the universe in general and with His people in particular. These expressions are very powerful extensions of God's personality. For example, God's *word* or speaking is not just an empty sound. It is dynamic and creative. As the Psalmist wrote, the whole universe came into being by His speaking: "By the word of the Lord were the heavens made, their starry host by the breath of His mouth" (Ps 33:6).

The same is true of the *spirit* of God. The Hebrew word sometimes translated spirit originally meant "movement of air." Though it sometimes means "wind" or "storm," most often it has the meaning of "breath." And the being that has "breath" is a living being. Applied to God it means that He is the *living* God, constantly reaching out in action.

It is no wonder that, later in the New Testament, these ideas serve as starting points for further development. Both John and Paul take up the idea of the *word* of God and apply it to Jesus Christ, while the idea of the *spirit* of God develops into a personal understanding of spirit: the Holy Spirit.

Each member of the Trinity is mentioned in the Old Testament. God the Father is mentioned in such pas-

51

sages as: "You, O Lord, are our Father, our Redeemer from of old is your name" (Isa 63:16), and "'You are my Father, my God, the Rock my Savior'" (Ps 89:26).

References to God the Son in his role as Messiah occur in verses such as: "'The days are coming,' declares the Lord, 'when I will raise up to David a righteous Branch, a King who will reign wisely and do what is just and right in the land. In His days Judah will be saved and Israel will live in safety. This is the name by which He will be called: the Lord Our Righteousness.'" (Jer 23:5-6); and "For to us a child is born, to us a son is given, and the government will be on His shoulders. And He will be called Wonderful Counselor, Mighty God" (Isaiah 9:6).

God the Holy Spirit is referred to in such passages as: "Now the earth was formless and empty, darkness was over the surface of the deep, and the Spirit of God was hovering over the waters" (Gen 1:2); and "Yet they rebelled and grieved His Holy Spirit" (Isa 63:10).

The Old Testament definitely provides a foreshadowing of the unity and diversity of God which is made more clear in the New Testament revelation of the Trinity.

NEW TESTAMENT REVELATION

Within God's word, it is in the New testament that the doctrine of the Trinity is most clearly taught. There are hints of it in the Old Testament, to be sure, but it was left to the New Testament for this precious doctrine to be clearly revealed.

The New Testament plainly teaches, as does the Old, that there is but one God, not three. New Testament passages such as Ephesians 4:4-6 and James 2:19

reveal the fact that "there is no God but one" (1 Cor 8:4). It is the united testimony of God's Word that there is only one God.

But the Bible also testifies, in both the Old and the New Testaments, that within the nature of the one God exist three distinct personalities: the Father, the Son, and the Holy Spirit. The New Testament also teaches that these three names are not synonymous, but represent three distinct and equal persons.

THE FATHER IS GOD

The New Testament talks about a person who is designated as the Father. This person is God. In passages such as John 6:27 and 1 Peter 1:2, He is called "God the Father." Jesus taught His disciples to pray, "Our Father in heaven" (Matt 6:9). And when Paul wrote to the Galatian Christians, he began his letter, "Paul, an apostle—sent not from men nor by man, but by Jesus Christ and God the Father, who raised Him from the dead" (Gal 1:1).

THE SON IS GOD

A second person the New Testament speaks of as God is Jesus, God the Son. The New Testament repeatedly affirms that Jesus Christ is God incarnate. He is set forth as the all-creative Word of God who actually is God (John 1:1-3). Other Scriptures ratifying Christ's full and essential deity include: Titus 2:13 in which Paul speaks of waiting "for the blessed hope—the glorious appearing of our great God and Savior, Jesus Christ"; and Hebrews 1:8 which quotes Psalm 45:6-7 as proof of the deity of Christ: "But about the Son He says, 'Your throne, O God, will last for ever and ever.'"

As Kenneth Boa elaborates, Christ's deity is proven by "the divine names given Him, by His works that only God could do, by His divine attributes (eternality, John 17:5; omnipresence, Matt. 28:20; omnipotence, Heb. 1:3; omniscience, Matt. 9:4), and by explicit statements of His deity (John 1:1; 20:28; Titus 2:13)."[3]

THE HOLY SPIRIT IS GOD

A third person spoken of in the New Testament as God is the Holy Spirit. In the following passage it becomes crystal clear that the Holy Spirit is deity: "'Ananias, how is it that Satan has so filled your heart that you have lied to the Holy Spirit?...You have not lied to men but to God" (Act 5:3-4).

Boa further notes that "the deity of the Holy Spirit can also be seen in the divine names used for Him (for example, 'the Spirit of our God,' 1 Cor. 6:11), in His attributes of deity (omnipresence, Ps. 139:7; omnipotence, Job 33:4; omniscience, 1 Cor. 2:10-12), and in His divine works (Gen. 1:2; Luke 1:35; John 3:5-6; 16:8; Rom. 8:26; 2 Tim. 3:16; 2 Peter 1:21)."[4]

These Scriptures, and others, prove beyond contradiction that the Father is God, the Son is God, and the Holy Spirit is God. The Father, the Son, and the Holy Spirit exist and have existed forever. Therefore, there was not a time when there was only the Father, then later the Son, and still later the Spirit.

Regarding the eternal nature of the Son of God, Billy Graham observes: "The Bible teaches that Jesus Christ had no beginning. He was never created. The Bible teaches that the heavens were created by Him (John 1:1-3). All the myriads of stars and flaming suns were created by Him. The earth was flung from His flaming fingertip. The birth of Jesus Christ that we celebrate at Christmas was not His beginning....The Bible only tells us, 'In the beginning was the Word, and the Word was with God, and the Word was God' (John 1:1)"[5]

The Son of God was preexistent before His entrance into the world as the child Jesus. According to Luke 1:34-35, when He was born of the virgin Mary, He had no human father, because His conception was caused by the miraculous power of the Holy Spirit. As John 1:14 points out, His birth was a change of condition, not a new beginning: "The Word became flesh and made His dwelling among us." The baby in the manger at Bethlehem was none other than the eternal Word of God!

Is there more than one God? As Josh McDowell and Don Stewart so aptly expressed it: "There is one God. This one God has a plural nature. This one God is called the Father, the Son, the Holy Spirit, all distinct personalities, all designated God. We are therefore led to the conclusion that the Father, Son, and Holy Spirit are one God, the doctrine of the Trinity."[6]

The doctrine of the Trinity points to the mystery of the Divine God whom Christians worship and serve. The doctrine has been regarded as basic to the Christian understanding of God's nature: in creeds and confessions of faith, Christian theologians have sought to bear witness to its truth; Christian musicians and artists have attempted to celebrate and illustrate its reality. And amid all their limitations of knowledge and understanding, Christians continue to worship and praise the Triune God—Father, Son, and Holy Spirit.

Dear friends, we know not what a day may bring forth. None of us knew that disaster would strike on September 11, and you don't know and neither do I, what will happen tomorrow. Yet we often live as if tomorrow is a sure thing. How easily we forget that "each man's life is but a breath" (Ps 39:50). We truly live a fragile, brief existence. The recent, tragic events have made us profoundly aware of how foolish it is to join with unbelievers who say, "Tomorrow will be like today, or even far better" (Isa 56:12).

Today, as we face uncertain times, how comforting it is for us to know the basic truth that we have a Triune God to whom we can turn for salvation. For Jesus said, "I am the way, and the truth, and the life. No one comes to the Father but through me" (John 14:6).

5

Where Is God?

How simple it would be for some people if just once they could see God! In fact, many men and women think it a bit unfair of God to keep Himself hidden, never allowing them a single glimpse, forcing them to grope their way as best they can toward an understanding of His nature.

In these perilous times, when people find themselves in a quandary because of the tremendous loss associated with the September 11 terrorist attacks and other events, it isn't too surprising that some of them may ask questions such as the following: Where is God? Why doesn't He intervene and make Himself obvious when tragedies like these occur? Why doesn't He speak aloud so we can hear Him? We need reassurance that He is really there. The natural world that we can hear and see and touch seems self-evident; the supernatural world, however, seems uncertain, and that is pretty unsettling.

What these people really want is proof! No wonder so many of them can readily identify with a phrase from a George Harrison song: "Oh sweet Lord, I really want to see you, I really want to be with you…" What they long for is to know they are in the actual presence of God Almighty.

It is difficult, isn't it, for us to answer the question "Where is God?", when we cannot see Him with our physical eyesight. We know from Scripture that our Lord is "the King eternal, immortal, invisible, the only God" (1 Tim 1:17). But *where* is He when we seem to need Him the most?

In theological terms we are talking about the omnipresence of God, the fact that He is present everywhere. Often the complaint of a busy person on a hectic day is: "I can't be in two places at the same time!" Of course, no man or woman can be anywhere except where he or she is. But God can, for He is not limited to any place. While it is inherent in our nature to be localized, to be "here" and not "there", it is inherent in His nature to be present in all places. Because "God is spirit" (John 4:24), He is present in His whole infinite deity at one and the same time everywhere.

Because God is everywhere, we cannot run away from Him, nor hide from His presence: "Where can I go from your Spirit? Where can I flee from your presence? If I go up to the heavens, you are there; if I make my bed in the depths, you are there. If I rise on the wings of the dawn, if I settle on the far side of the sea, even there your hand will guide me, your right hand will hold me fast" (Ps 139:7-10). When the Psalmist asks "Where?", the answer is: "You are there." Although we can't see Him with our physical eyes, God is really there.

But how can He be everywhere at once and still be a real person as we are? Our finite minds are controlled by a three-dimensional world. But God lives in another dimension different from nature as we know it, a supernatural or spiritual dimension. So God is not just quantitatively bigger than the universe He created, His mode of existence is qualitatively different from that of the universe.

This is difficult for us to imagine. It is like describing a Mozart symphony to a person born deaf or autumn colors to a person born blind. To help us appreciate the problem, Philip Yancey offers the following: Imagine yourself trying to communicate with a creature on a microscope slide. The 'universe' to such a creature consists of only two dimensions, the flat plane of the glass slide; its senses cannot perceive anything beyond the edges. How could you convey a concept of space or height or depth to such a creature? Looking 'from above,' you can understand the creature's two-dimensional world as well as the three-dimensional world surrounding it. The creature, however, 'from below,' can only comprehend a world of two dimensions. In a similar way, the unseen world exists outside our range of perception—except for rare interventions into our 'plane,' which we call miracles."[1]

The Word of God points to a realm beyond nature itself, to a supernatural or spiritual dimension we cannot see with our physical eyes except on special occasions of miraculous modification. God lives on that "higher" level, in another spatial dimension. He is present everywhere even though we puny creatures "here below" cannot physically see nor logically comprehend the nature of another dimension with our present faculties. Yet we Christians know that God is there, for we have experienced Him in our lives.

GOD IS TRANSCENDENT

While affirming the omnipresence of God, we must not make the mistake of identifying the material universe with God. For God is not a part of the universe but its Creator.

Scripture makes it quite clear that God created everything there is by the word of his mouth: "By the word of the Lord were the heavens made, their starry host by the breath of His mouth....For He spoke, and it came to be; He commanded, and it stood firm" (Ps 33:6,9); "By faith we understand that the universe was formed at God's command, so that what is seen was not made out of what was visible" (Heb 11:3).

God, the Creator of the Universe, is not a part of nature. As Kenneth Boa explains: "We must be careful to distinguish the doctrine of the divine presence from the error of pantheism. Pantheism fails to distinguish the created from the Creator because it says that God is nature and nature is God. On the other hand, the Bible teaches that though God is present everywhere, He is not resident in everything. God fills the heavens and the earth, but the things in the heavens and the earth shouldn't be called God. When you pick up a book or lean against a tree you are not touching God as the pantheist would assert."[2]

Just as a potter who makes a vase, a carpenter who builds a house, and an artist who paints a picture are all distinct from what they have created, so too, God who made the universe is distinct from it. Only a God who is transcendent, apart from what He has made, can be the Creator and sustainer of the vast universe we know.

GOD IS IMMANENT

Although God is separate from nature, He is not absent from His creation, however. Deism falsely teaches that God is Creator of the universe but not actively involved in its present life. But the creation is not a clock which God made, wound up, and now leaves ticking. God did not simply create the universe and then withdraw to see what would happen.

God is immanent, present in his creation, in certain very real and definite ways: "God so made the universe that it is totally dependent on His power at every moment to stay intact and in motion. God can exist without the universe but the universe cannot exist without Him. He is in it as its upholder, sustainer and energizer, giving it continued existence and operating the laws of nature. So, for instance, season follows season and the plant grows from the seed."[3] God not only created the universe, but also sustains "all things by His powerful word" (Heb 1:3).

Scripture continually emphasizes the immanence of God: He provides food for the birds of the air, and He beautifully clothes the lilies of the field (Matt 6:26-29); He determines the number of the stars, makes the grass grow, and provides food for the cattle (Ps 147:4-9). Acts 17:28 also speaks clearly about God's immanence, for "in Him we live and move and have our being." And immanence is shown too in God's intimate dealings with all people: "For a man's ways are in full view of the Lord, and He examines all his paths" (Prov 5:21).

The fact that "He knows the secrets of the heart" (Ps 44:21) can be comforting or disquieting depending on one's relation to the Lord. But for those who are rightly related to God there is real peace and comfort in His presence because nothing at all can separate Christians from God's love: "For I am convinced that neither death nor life, neither angels nor demons, neither the present nor the future, nor any powers, neither height nor depth, nor anything else in all creation, will be able to separate us from the love of God that is in Christ Jesus our Lord" (Rom 8:38-39).

God is everywhere present in the universe, but He is nevertheless separated from it by an unbridgeable gap. God is both immanent within His works and transcendent above them. He is intimate and separate; near yet far: "I live in a high and holy place, but also with him who is contrite and lowly in spirit" (Isa 57:15). As Augustine so aptly stated, God is "nearer than hands and feet." Or as Luther put it: "God is closer to everything than anything is to itself."

God's Word teaches two important truths concerning His relation to the universe: first, His transcendence, His separation and exaltation above the universe and man (Isa 6:1); second, His immanence, His presence in the world and nearness to man (Eph 4:6). God is not so far above us that He is not touched by our sorrows and tears.

OMNIPRESENCE AND LOCALIZED PRESENCE

The Word of God tells us that God's presence is everywhere in the universe, for all three members of the Godhead are omnipresent. The Father's universal presence is declared in Jeremiah 23:24: "Do not I fill heaven and earth?" The Son's presence everywhere is propounded in ephesians 1:23 which states: "[Christ] fills everything in every way." And the Holy Spirit's omnipresence is evident in Psalms 139:7 which asks: "Where can I go from your Spirit? Where can I flee from your presence?"

All three persons are present in all places as one God, for there is no place where one person is present without the other two being there also.

The whole of God is present in all places at once, yet Scripture also teaches that each member of the Trinity can be localized in specific places. Throughout the ages the invisible God has manifested himself in visible form. It must be remembered, however, that this is an appearance of God in some form to the outward senses, not God in His real essence.

LOCALIZED PRESENCE OF GOD THE FATHER

Let's look at the specially localized presence of God the Father. Although our Father God in His omnipresence fills the universe (Jer 23:24), in His manifest presence He sits on his throne in heaven (Isa 6:1). The Bible teaches that God's throne in heaven is the localized center of His sovereignty. Although the language used to describe it is usually figurative and anthropomorphic, God's heavenly abode is indeed a real place. The three members of the trinity are there along with a vast number of angels and a host of redeemed people (Heb 12:22-23).

Heaven constitutes a special localization of God, and a number of Old and New Testament passages mention heaven and God's throne. In his vision of God, Isaiah "saw the Lord seated on a throne, high and exalted, and the train of His robe filled the temple" (Isa 6:1). John also recorded his vision of God: "At once I was in the Spirit, and there before me was a throne in heaven with someone sitting on it. And the one who sat there had the appearance of jasper and carnelian. A rainbow, resembling an emerald, encircled the throne" (Rev 4:2-3). Other passages include: Psalms 103:19; Matt 6:9; and Hebrews 8:1.

Scripture is also replete with examples of manifestations of God on earth. In the Old Testament, reference is made to God meeting with His people in particular places, such as: in a bright cloud of glory; at the tent in the wilderness; at the temple. For example, the Word of God tells us that when Solomon built the temple, "the glory of the Lord filled it" (2 Chr 7:2). The glory of God's presence in the temple is an instance of God's special localized presence on earth. Of course, from the standpoint of God's omnipresence, Solomon knew that the temple he had just finished could not contain God: "But will God really dwell on the earth? The heavens, even the highest heaven, cannot contain you. How much less this temple I have built!" (1 Kings 8:27). Yet from the standpoint of localized presence, God was able to dwell in the most holy place in the temple. However, the glory of God's manifest presence in the temple later departed because of the iniquity of the Israelites (Ezek 10:3-4, 18-19; 11:22-23).

LOCALIZED PRESENCE OF God the SON

Although Jesus Christ is omnipresent, He is also specially localized. Christ in His omnipresence is present with His church everywhere (Matt 28:20), but in His manifest presence lived in Palestine while on earth, sits now at the right hand of God the Father in heaven (Heb 8:1), and will appear to all as the glorified God-man at His Second Coming (Rev 1:7).

Scripture says that God assumed a divine-human nature in the incarnation of Jesus Christ: "The Word became flesh and made His dwelling among us" (John 1:14). Christ's incarnation is the only time God became flesh and lived with mankind.

By the incarnation, Jesus Christ entered into our little world in a truly unique way, emptying Himself of the advantages of deity, submitting Himself to the conditions of humanity: "Christ Jesus, who, being in very nature God, did not consider equality with God something to be grasped, but made Himself nothing, taking the very nature of a servant, being made in human likeness. And being found in appearance as a man, He humbled Himself and became obedient to death—even death on a cross!" (Phil 2:5-8).

After the resurrection, Christ took on a new body of glorified flesh suitable for a heavenly existence (See 1 Cor 15:42-51). He is still localized in His resplendent resurrection body "at the right hand of the throne of the Majesty in heaven" (Heb 8:1). And, at His second coming, Jesus will appear to everyone as the glorified God-man: "Look, He is coming in the clouds, and every eye will see Him" (Rev 1:7). What a wonderful day that will be!

LOCALIZED PRESENCE OF GOD THE HOLY SPIRIT

Even though the Holy Spirit in His omnipresence is present everywhere (Ps 139:7), in His manifest presence He resides in heaven, the seat of God's throne (Ps 139:8). The Holy Spirit is localized too in the sense that He indwells the physical bodies of individual Christians (1 Cor 6:19) and the Christian community as "a holy temple" (Eph 2:20-21).

Also, as Mark 1:10-11 relates, the Holy Spirit was localized in symbolic form at the baptism of Jesus: "As Jesus was coming up out of the water, He saw heaven being torn open and the Spirit descending on Him like a dove. And a voice came from heaven: 'You are my Son, whom I love; with you I am well pleased.'"

And, as Acts 2:1-4 informs, the Holy Spirit was also localized in symbolic manner to the first Christians on the day of Pentecost: "They were all together in one place. Suddenly a sound like the blowing of a violent wind came from heaven and filled the whole house where they were sitting. They saw what seemed to be tongues of fire that separated and came to rest on each of them. All of them were filled with the Holy Spirit."

The coming of God's Son made possible the indwelling of God in believers who trust in Christ's name. "Repent and believe the good news!" (Mark 1:15)—that is the condition on which the presence of God becomes real to mankind. For the nearness of God realizes itself only through our repentant and believing acceptance of God's Son. Therefore, God does not indwell all people: He indwells believers, but not the unredeemed.

The Father sent the Holy Spirit in Christ's name, and now He is indwelling believers on earth, teaching and guiding them (John 14:26). Jesus said that the Holy Spirit would be a great inner source of life to believers (John 7:38-39). He also said that the Holy Spirit would convict the world concerning sin (John 16:8), guide Christians into all truth (John 16:13), glorify Jesus in our midst (John (16:14), empower us to be Christ's witnesses (Acts 1:8), and join us in bearing that testimony (John 15:26).

In summary, the Holy Spirit is omnipresent in such a way that He is wholly present everywhere. Yet He is also localized in that He indwells Christians and resides in His ultimate dwelling place in heaven, the center of God's dominion.

THE RELEVANCE OF GOD'S OMNIPRESENCE

The biblical concept of a God so great He is present everywhere has real significance for all people. Nearly three thousand years ago the psalmist asked: "When I consider your heavens, the work of your fingers, the moon and the stars, which you have set in place, what is man that you are mindful of him?" (Ps 8:3-4). Job asked a similar question: "What is man that you make so much of him, that you give him so much attention?" (Job 7:17).

Today some men and women voice a contemporary version of the same question: What does God care about this little planet of ours compared with the vastness of the universe? Or, as a medical doctor, hearing of the results of the Hubble telescope probe of the universe, recently queried: "The pictures from the Hubble telescope were jammed with stars. After appropriate calculations, the researchers concluded that there are probably about 50 billion galaxies in the universe....I am humbled and troubled by the enormity of this discovery. ...Is it any longer appropriate to ask God to find a parking space at the mall, and then thank Him when you do? Does each death in the world make any imprint whatsoever on the Universe as a whole? With so much chance for extra-terrestrial life, can we afford to be so smug about being special and unique?"[4]

Compared to the vastness of God's creation, mankind is nothing at all: even our galaxy is only a speck among billions. Yet man is significant in the eyes of our Creator. The Bible tells us that one of the reasons God created the splendors of the universe was in order to reveal "His eternal power and divine nature" (Rom 1:20) to mankind.

But why is our lilliputian planet and those who inhabit it of such infinite value to God? Part of the problem is solved when we consider that size means little to God. Although the earth is a minute speck in the vastness of God's creation, it is on *this* planet that the principal program of God's plan is coming to fruition.

If it seems unbelievable that God would center His plan on our tiny planet, how much more incredible is it that He would actually send His beloved Son to die in our place! Jesus created this immense universe with its numberless galaxies and stars (John 1:10), and yet He loved us enough to humble Himself, become man, and pay for our sins with His own blood: "He was pierced for our transgressions, He was crushed for our iniquities; the punishment that brought us peace was upon Him, and by his wounds we are healed" (Isa 53:5).

Where is God? In Jesus Christ, God came close. His life answered the questions: Is God hidden? Is God silent? As the New Testament tells it, God loudly broke His silence while Jesus lived here on earth. With Jesus, God took on a physical shape we could hear and see and touch: "That which was from the beginning, which we have heard, which we have seen with our eyes, which we have looked at and our hands have touched—this we proclaim concerning the Word of life" (1 John 1:1).

With Jesus, the longing of human hearts actually to see God was satisfied. Because of the incarnation we can see what otherwise was hidden, for when Christ became flesh and made His dwelling among us, we beheld "His glory, the glory of the One and Only, who came from the Father, full of grace and truth" (John 1:14).

The more we contemplate the stupendous greatness of God's creation, the more we can really begin to appreciate the shame and condescension Christ bore for us. The entrance of Christ into unglorified humanity was the supreme picture of His humility and love, illustrating the extent to which the Son of God was willing to go to become our Redeemer and demonstrating God's grace and mercy (John 3:16) in fulfilling His promise of salvation. What a wonderful, loving God we have!

"Blessed be your glorious name, and may it be exalted above all blessing and praise. You alone are the Lord. You made the heavens, even the highest heavens, and all their starry host, the earth and all that is on it, the seas and all that is in them. You give life to everything, and the multitudes of heaven worship you" (Neh 9:5-6).

"Sing to the Lord, all the earth; proclaim His salvation day after day. Declare His glory among the nations, His marvelous deeds among all peoples. For great is the Lord and most worthy of praise" (1 Chr 16:23-25).

6

How Powerful Is God?

In the season of our insecurity after recent
terrorist events, we feel vulnerable and weak. We
wonder if God is powerful enough to take us through
this present, dreadful storm. In addition, queries concerning God's power arise in our minds in regard to
other concerns such as: Is God powerful enough to heal
my illness? Can He put my marriage back together?
Can He help me to be more secure financially? Can He
stop an earthquake or storm or flood from happening in
my community? Countless questions of this nature arise
in the minds of men and women everywhere. How
powerful is God in situations such as these? In order to
understand God's power, we need to see what Scripture
teaches about the power of God.

A BIBLICAL DEFINITION

In the Bible the infinite power of God is expressed
well by one of His names—Almighty. When God
appeared to Abraham to announce His covenant, He
referred to Himself as "God Almighty" (Gen 17:1).
Revelation 19:6-7 likewise testifies of God's supreme
power: "For our Lord God Almighty reigns. Let us
rejoice and be glad and give Him glory!" In fact, scholars tell us that the Old Testament word for "Almighty"
(*Shaday*) and the New Testament word (*Pantokrator*)

collectively appear 56 times in the Bible.[1] In describing God's power, the Bible also uses such words as strength, might, authority, and ability, in addition to certain human characteristics ascribed to God.

In a biblical definition of God's omnipotence, at least three concepts are involved: (1) God can do all things; (2) nothing is too hard for God to do; and (3) God has an inexhaustible supply of power. Each concept contributes to our understanding and helps us answer the question "How powerful is God?" Therefore, let us look at each of these concepts individually, so that we might understand them more clearly.

GOD CAN DO ALL THINGS .

The Word of God frequently affirms the fact that "with God all things are possible" (Matt 19:26). In his bitter experience, Job's reply to God's evaluation of his situation was: "I know that you can do all things; no plan of yours can be thwarted" (Job 42:2). And the Bible tells us that God's power holds true both in the experience of mankind and in that of the heavenly inhabitants: "He does as He pleases with the powers of heaven and the peoples of the earth" (Dan 4:35).

While such statements attest to God's total ability, they also suggest that God's purpose controls His power. Therefore, the Bible teaches that God can do anything and everything, but only when such actions are in accordance with His will and purpose.

NOTHING IS TOO HARD FOR GOD TO DO

Biblical testimony of God's omnipotence was offered in prayer by Jeremiah: "Ah, Sovereign Lord, you have made the heavens and the earth by your great

power and outstretched arm. Nothing is too hard for
you" (Jer 32:17). Praise for God's power was also
presented in song by a psalmist: "Shout with joy to God,
all the earth! Sing the glory of His name; make His
praise glorious! Say to God, 'How awesome are your
deeds! So great is your power that your enemies cringe
before you. All the earth bows down to you; they sing
praise to you, they sing praise to your name'" (Ps 66:1-
4).

Scripture affirms that nothing is too difficult for
God to do. But can He really do everything? Can God
do anything evil? Can He do something self-contradic-
tory? Can He deny himself? As Don Stewart points out,
"God cannot do the logically or actually impossible. He
cannot contradict His nature or character. That is not
within the realm of His power. Thus there are limits to
what God can do."[2]

However, God is capable of doing everything that
is logically possible and consistent with His will and
nature. William Rowe includes all the necessary qualifi-
cations in defining omnipotence to mean that "God can
do anything that is an absolute possibility (i.e., is logically possible) and not inconsistent with any of His basic
attributes."[3] It is evident that the Lord will not do things
that are contrary to His character and purposes.

GOD HAS AN INEXHAUSTIBLE SUPPLY OF POWER

No matter how physically conditioned a man or
woman may be, he or she will eventually get tired by the
continual exercise of strength. We over-fifty folks
especially know this to be true. When we go for daily
walks, our old knees do not move as they once did. We
can't go as fast or as long, and our bodies ache more.
Younger guys or girls may give us a condescending

smile that seems to suggest we are too old and should perhaps retire to the wheelchair crowd.

Even youngsters eventually get tired, however. But God never does. He has an inexhaustible supply of power: "Do you not know? Have you not heard? The Lord is the everlasting God, the Creator of the ends of the earth. He will not grow tired or weary...He gives strength to the weary and increases the power of the weak. Even youths grow tired and weary, and young men stumble and fall; but those who hope in the Lord will renew their strength" (Isa 40:28-31).

God not only never grows weary in the exercise of His power, He never needs to sleep either. Psalm 121:1-4 shares the significance of that truth: "I lift up my eyes to the hills—where does my help come from? My help comes from the Lord, the Maker of heaven and earth. He will not let your foot slip—He who watches over you will not slumber; indeed, He who watches over Israel will neither slumber nor sleep."

We can have confidence in a God who never grows weary or tired, for our faith is grounded in the wonderful knowledge of His unlimited power which knows no bounds.

In attempting to define the omnipotence of God, we have looked at three concepts: (1) God can do all things; (2) nothing is too hard for God to do; and (3) God has an inexhaustible supply of power.

Definitions are helpful, but the full impact of those definitions is best felt when we see the actual evidence of God's power. So what kinds of things does God do which display what our definition has told us?

God realized that people need proof; consequently, He has often revealed His omnipotence through acts such as the following: (1) His creation of all things; (2) His providential care; (3) His control of governments;

(4) His mighty acts; and (5) His conversions of women and men.

His Creation of All Things

The power of God is clearly portrayed on the canvas of the created world: "For since the creation of the world God's invisible qualities—His eternal power and divine nature—have been clearly seen, being understood from what has been made" (Rom 1:20). With one look at the expanse of the skies, the vastness of the oceans, or the beauty of a sunset we quickly understand something of the awesome power of God.

Scripture informs us that God founded the heavens and the earth and all that is in it: "God said, 'Let there be'...And it was so" (Gen 1); "Thus the heavens and the earth were completed in all their vast array" (Gen 2:1).

Before we mortals can work, we must have both materials and tools. But the startling thing about the Creation is that God made the universe without the use of previously existing materials and spoke it into existence: "By faith we understand that the universe was formed at God's command, so that what is seen was not made out of what was visible" (Heb 11:3). Now that's what I call power!

God not only created the universe, but also sustains it, for "in Him all things hold together" (Col 1:17). Hebrews 1:3 adds that He sustains "all things by His powerful word." Thus, the Word of God teaches that God manifests His power in the laws of the universe which keep the cosmos operating in an orderly, harmonious fashion. If God were to remove His sustaining hand, the universe would disintegrate into utter chaos and disorder.

HIS PROVIDENTIAL CARE

God's power is the attribute that meets the needs of all creatures: "You open your hand and satisfy the desires of every living thing" (Ps 145:16); "These all look to you to give them their food at the proper time. When you give it to them, they gather it up; when you open your hand, they are satisfied with good things (Ps 104:27-28).

If God had a limit to His strength, we might well despair. But since He is clothed with omnipotence, no need is too great for Him to supply, no temptation too powerful for Him to deliver from, no prayer too difficult for Him to answer: "Now to Him who is able to do immeasurably more than we ask or imagine, according to His power that is at work within us, to Him be glory in the church and in Christ Jesus throughout all genera-tion, for ever and ever! Amen" (Eph 3:20-21).

HIS CONTROL OF GOVERNMENTS

God possesses control and sovereignty over all governments: "Everyone must submit himself to the governing authorities, for there is no authority except that which God has established. The authorities that exist have been established by God" (Rom 13:1).

Civil authority of every type comes from the Lord. Even the kingdom of evil power, headed by Satan, is subject to control by God. As noted in Job 1, God is Almighty and Satan can do nothing without His permis-sion

Arthur W. Pink has this to say about God's author-ity over every form of government: "Take his restraining of the malice of Satan. 'The devil, as a roaring lion, walketh about, seeking whom he may devour' (1 Peter

5:8). He is filled with hatred against God and with fiendish enmity against men, particularly the saints....Could he have his will, he would treat all the same way he treated Job....But, little as men may realize it, God bridles him to a large extent, prevents him from carrying out his evil designs, and confines him within *His* ordinations....So too God restrains the natural corruption of men. He suffers sufficient outbreakings of sin to show what fearful havoc has been wrought by man's apostasy from his Maker, but who can conceive the frightful lengths to which men would go were God to remove His curbing hand?"[4]

Although evil men may choose to commit horrible atrocities such as Hitler's attempted extermination of Jews during the Holocaust and Osama bin Laden's terrorist attacks and murders of innocent civilians in present times, God restrains the freedom of choice of wicked men such as these by eventually bringing them to justice in one way or another. In this way God limits destructiveness and brings judgment to leaders and nations. God's curbing hand will prevail as He leads the United States and our allies in the great struggle against the evil that has been perpetrated against us.

His Mighty Acts

Another factor displaying God's power is His mighty acts or miracles. Miracles occur when God interrupts the ordinary course of nature for a specific purpose.

In the Old Testament, the standard of God's power is the miraculous deliverance of Israel from Egypt. In later centuries, the prophets continually reminded the people of the great Exodus and of the miracles accompanying it. These prophets recognized God as the Lord "who brought the Israelites up out of Egypt" (Jer 16:14).

Just as the Exodus was the standard of God's power in the Old Testament, the resurrection of Jesus Christ was the measure of power in the New Testament, for our Lord "was declared with power to be the Son of God by His resurrection from the dead" (Rom 1:4).

Before His death and resurrection, Jesus revealed the power of God through such miracles as His casting out of evil spirits (Mark 5:1-20), His healing of all manner of sickness (Mark 6:53-56), His provision of bread for the crowds (Mark 6:30-44), His calming of the storm (Mark 4:35-41), and His walking on the water (Mark 6:45-52).

He also demonstrated God's omnipotence by His power over death in the cases of Lazarus (John 11:38-44), of the son of the widow from Nain (Luke 7:11-17), and of the daughter of Jairus (Mark 5:35-43). But God's glorious power was supremely illustrated in His own resurrection from the dead.

Past evidences of God's power should build our confidence in the power of God for the future. God's Word teaches that His power will be mightily displayed once again, as it was over 3,000 years ago in Egypt. In the last days, the entire world will be affected by catastrophic events whose only explanation will be the mighty power of God. The last book of the Bible predicts these events and reveals that the people of earth will know that God is showing His power through the terrible plagues, yet large numbers will refuse "to repent and glorify Him" (Rev 16:9). They are like present day people whom some of us know, who despite the collapse of their own lives, continue to reject God's loving provision for their salvation.

Although true miracles are a demonstration of God's power, they do not always convince people. Though people everywhere in the last times will see stupendous examples of God's miraculous acts, many still will not believe in Him.

HIS CONVERSIONS OF WOMEN AND MEN

It is the omnipotence of God which makes conversions possible, because the power of God is contained in the gospel "for the salvation of everyone who believes" (Rom 1:16). This is why the Bible tells us that God accomplishes His purpose through the power of His word: "My word that goes out from my mouth: it will not return to me empty, but will accomplish what I desire and achieve the purpose for which I sent it (Isa 55:11).

Out of His great wisdom and love, God devised and made possible the free gift of our salvation. And this power of God which made possible our conversion is the same power which enables us to triumph over sin and temptation in this present life (Rom 8:1-8; 15:13). Our spiritual life then is begun and maintained by the omnipotence of God.

In addition, we are kept secure in our salvation by the power of God: "For I am convinced that neither death nor life, neither angels nor demons, neither the present nor the future, nor any powers, neither height nor depth, nor anything else in all creation, will be able to separate us from the love of God that is in Christ Jesus our Lord" (Rom 8:38-39). Now that is security! Nothing, absolutely nothing, can separate us from the love of God in Christ Jesus!

In chapter six we examined evidence of God's omnipotence as exhibited in His power to create the universe, to provide for all life, to control governments, to perform mighty acts, and to convert women and men.

How powerful is God? It is a comfort to know that God is in ultimate control of all situations. Disease may strike our mortal bodies, but God is powerful enough to heal through treatment by doctors and medicine and, at times, through miraculous intervention. Other times, God may provide ultimate healing by taking His children home to be with Him. Marriages may falter, but God is strong enough to put back together marriages of individuals who truly care about one another and who really desire reconciliation. God knows what is best in each situation, so there are times when divorce is the only answer.

Concerning America's present difficulties, wicked men have attempted to terrorize America, but God's restraining hand will prevail as He assists our Government and our military forces in the fight against terrorism. Because God is sovereign over all, we can know that evil will ultimately be defeated. Our Lord is definitely the Almighty God!

7

What Does God Know?

Does God know everything, or are there things which are beyond His knowledge? For instance, after the September 11 terrorist attacks occurred, some people asked, "Did this take God by surprise? Did He know in advance that this horrible atrocity was going to occur?" Other types of questions surface, such as: Does God know about the hidden difficulties we sometimes face? Does He know about sinful thoughts or secret deeds? Conversely, when an individual's reputation is falsely maligned, does He know that person's true character? And does He know about the joys, the sorrows, and the trials we may face in the future? These are just a few examples of questions relating to God's knowledge that people, young and old, struggle with today.

In theological terminology, Divine omniscience means that the range of God's knowledge is total: "God is greater than our hearts, and He knows everything" (1 John 3:20). Thus, the Bible clearly teaches that God knows all things, that nothing is hidden from His omniscient gaze.

Concerning the knowledge of God, Arthur W. Pink writes: "God is omniscient. He knows everything:

81

everything possible, everything actual; all events and all creatures, of the past, the present, and the future. He is perfectly acquainted with every detail in the life of every being in heaven, in earth, and in hell....Nothing escapes His notice, nothing can be hidden from Him, nothing is forgotten by Him....His knowledge is perfect."[1]

Some further characteristics of God's omniscience include the following: (1) God's knowledge is accurate; (2) God's knowledge is advanced; (3) God's knowledge is universal; (4) God's knowledge is infinite; and (5) God's knowledge is incomparable. To better understand these characteristics let us look at them individually.

GOD'S KNOWLEDGE IS ACCURATE

God's knowledge is without error, for He knows our hearts, our frames, our needs, and our pathways.

First, Scripture states that God "knows the secrets of the heart" (Ps 44:21). This applies to all people because "the eyes of the Lord are everywhere, keeping watch on the wicked and the good" (Prov 15:3).

Because God's knowledge is accurate concerning the heart, Jesus had something to say to the hypocritical Pharisees, the first century religious sect whose members outwardly justified themselves by strict adherence to manmade laws but inwardly retained gross violations of God given laws: "You are the ones who justify yourselves in the eyes of men, but God knows your hearts. What is highly valued among men is detestable in God's sight" (Luke 16:15).

When it comes to sinful thoughts and secret deeds, God knows: "You know my folly, O God; my guilt is not hidden from you" (Ps 69:5); "You have set our iniquities before you, our secret sins in the light of your presence" (Ps 90:8). No act—good or bad—escapes the all-seeing eye of our omniscient God. God truly knows our hearts. Today, terrorists may endeavor to escape justice, but God knows their wicked schemes and will surely bring them to account for what they have done: "The wicked plot against the righteous and gnash their teeth at them. The Lord laughs at the wicked, for He knows their day is coming" (Ps 37:12-13).

Second, God knows our frames. To the Christian, God's omniscience is a truth providing much comfort. In times of perplexity and weakness, we assure ourselves that God remembers our frames: "For He knows how we are formed, He remembers that we are dust" (Ps 103:14).

God knows exactly what we are like: "O Lord, you have searched me and you know me. You know when I sit and when I rise; you perceive my thoughts from afar. You discern my going out and my lying down; you are familiar with all my ways. Before a word is on my tongue you know it completely, O Lord" (Ps 139:1-4).

God definitely knows all about us! Yet, thanks to his patience and mercy, He still loves and accepts His children. Because of our faith in Jesus Christ, we are accepted and loved by God, for when we accept Christ by faith, turning to Him in sorrow and repentance for our sins, we thereby escape judgment.

God also knows our needs, for your Father in heaven "knows what you need before you ask Him" (Matt 6:8). God's knowledge, though great enough to know the stars by number, is yet personal enough to be aware of all your needs: "Therefore I tell you, do not worry about your life, what you will eat or drink; or about your body, what you will wear. Is not life more important than food, and the body more important than clothes? Look at the birds of the air; they do not sow or reap or store away in barns, and yet your heavenly

Father feeds them. Are you not much more valuable than they?...So do not worry...But seek first His kingdom and His righteousness, and all these things will be given to you as well" (Matt 6:25-26, 31, 33).

This special sermon by Jesus emphasizes that material needs do not represent the true priorities. God knows all about our earthly needs anyway. So we can dispense with undue concern about physical matters and concentrate on spiritual concerns instead. We can follow the injunction of Christ's sermon to seek first His kingdom and His righteousness, then God will take care of our temporal needs.

A fourth thing God knows is our pathways. All men and women need direction. But where do we get guidance to know what to do, where to go, and how to do it? Questions like these loom large in our minds: Should I go to a certain school? Should I marry a particular person? Should I take a certain job? Life is certainly filled with the need for guidance.

But don't despair! God has promised direction and guidance: "I will instruct you and teach you in the way you should go; I will counsel you and watch over you" (Ps 32:8); "Commit your way to the Lord; trust in Him and He will do this" (Ps 37:5).

An omniscient God can arrange for our lives and direct our pathways: "The Lord will guide you always; He will satisfy your needs in a sun-scorched land and will strengthen your frame. You will be like a well-watered garden, like a spring whose waters never fail" (Isa 58:11).

GOD'S KNOWLEDGE IS ADVANCED

God knows the future in advance because He is not subject to time as we are. He is not bound to the past-present-future structure which dominates our lives. There is a time line on which we are born into the world and are carried along by the events of life until we die. But, as John R. Rice notes, the Lord who is presented in the Bible is outside time: "With God there is no past or future, but an eternal present. Before the world began, He knew every person who would be born and what they would do. The future He knows perfectly; the past He remembers perfectly. The past is as clear to God as the present. But the future is also as clear as the present. So before the world began, God gave His Son, and in the mind and plan of God, Christ was a Lamb slain before the foundation of the world (Rev. 13:8)."[2]

God's knowledge of all things past, present, and future has been likened to a motion picture: "If we watch a movie we see the frames in sequence, so it looks as if Act 2 follows Act 1 and Act 3 follows Act 2. We see what looks like consecutive action. But if you were to take that same piece of film and hang it up on the wall, you could see the end, the beginning, and the middle all at once."[3] We see history like a sequence of still frames, one following another, but God sees the entire "movie" at once. Therefore, strictly speaking, God does not "foresee" the future, he simply sees everything in a timeless present. God knows all things because He exists in the eternal now.

God's knowledge of the future is illustrated in every prophecy recorded in Scripture. The Old Testament contains hundreds of predictions concerning the history of Israel which were fulfilled in detail centuries after they were made. So too, it includes hundreds of prophecies foretelling Christ's earthly career which were also accomplished in minutest detail. These biblical predictions are not vague prophecies but very specific

God-directed prophetic statements which cannot be accounted for by chance or collusion.

For example, evidence shows that the Old Testament prophets testified to the coming of Christ the Messiah hundreds of years before His birth. How do we know this? Bible scholars know this to be true because the Old Testament was completed around 350 years before Jesus of Nazareth was even born!

The following list of some Old Testament predictions and New Testament fulfillments regarding the person of Jesus Christ demonstrate how thoroughly His coming was foretold: (1) born of a virgin (Isa 7:14; Matt 1:18-25); (2) of the house of David (2 Sam 7:12; Jer 23:5; Matt 1:1; Luke 1:32); (3) born in Bethlehem (Micah 5:2; Matt 2:1; Luke 2;4-7); (4) anointed by the Holy Spirit (Isa 11:2; Matt 3:16-17); (5) preaching ministry (Isa 61:1-3; Luke 4:17-21); (6) triumphal entry (Zech 9:9; John 12:12-16); (7) betrayal price (Zech 11:12-13; Matt 26:15; 27:7-10); (8) beaten and spat upon (Isa 50:6; Matt 26:67); (9) mocked (Ps 22:7-8; Luke 23:35); (10) hands and feet pierced (Ps 22:16; John 19:16-18); (11) crucified with transgressors (Isa 53:12; Mark 15:27-28); (12) lots cast for His garments (Ps 22:18; John 19:23-24); (13) cry from the cross (Ps 22:1; Matt 27:46); (14) buried with the rich (Isa 53:9; Matt 27:57-60); (20) resurrection and exaltation (Ps 16:10; Isa 52:13; 53:10-12; Acts 2:25-32).

The odds that one person could fulfill these specific Messianic prophecies by chance are astronomical! Yet Jesus of Nazareth fulfilled these and many more.

In like manner, the Old and New Testaments contain many other prophecies yet future, and they too "must be fulfilled" (Luke 24:44), for they rest on the knowledge of Him who knows "the end from the beginning, from ancient times, what is still to come" (Isa 46:10).

In regard to God knowing the future, questions such as the following trouble many people: If God is all-knowing and completely sovereign, then how can we humans have free will? Doesn't God have to work everything out in advance?

The relationship between the knowledge and sovereignty of God and the freedom and responsibility of humans has perplexed theologians throughout the ages. On the one hand, the Bible clearly teaches that God is sovereign. On the other hand, Scripture also teaches the truth that we are really free and responsible human beings.

And therein lies the difficulty. There seems to be a tension between two seemingly irreconcilable points: the knowledge and sovereignty of God and the freedom and responsibility of human beings. How do we answer such questions?

Again, it is helpful to see God as outside time. As mentioned earlier, all things are eternally present to God—all events of the past, the present, and the future. A.W. Tozer phrased it so beautifully: "In one unified present glance He comprehends all things from everlasting, and the flutter of a seraph's wings a thousand ages hence is seen by Him now without moving His eyes"[4]

Accordingly, as far as God is concerned, all things have been known to Him always, for there is no beginning or end of His knowledge. But God's foreknowledge of how a person will use his free will does not dictate that person's choice. God foresees but does not necessitate or control the actions of free human beings.

Referring to 2 Timothy 4:10, Paul E. Little explains that "God's foreknowledge is not in itself the *cause* of what happens. For example, God foreknew that Demas would forsake the Apostle Paul for love of this world, but God's foreknowledge did not *predispose* Demas to turn back, much less *compel* him to do so. Demas acted in freedom; he made his own personal choice, under no compulsion. Again, God foreknew that Saul would receive Christ and become Paul the Apostle, but on the Damascus Road Saul exercised his own will in answering the Lord's summons. God foreknows your decisions before you make them—He knows what you will do and where you will go—but this foreknowledge does not interfere in the slightest with your complete freedom to act."[5]

Divine foreknowledge is practiced by a timeless God, but His advance knowledge in no way lessens our freedom, our privilege, or our responsibility to make correct moral choices or to come to know him.

The two threads of God's sovereignty and human choice are inextricably interwoven. But, no matter how hard we try, we still cannot understand how these threads fit together, because they go beyond the boundaries of our human understanding. This shouldn't surprise us, however. When we start talking about God's truth, it is understandable that some parts would be mystery.

J.I. Packer calls this difficulty of reconciling divine sovereignty and human freedom an antinomy, an apparent contradiction between conclusions that seem equally logical or necessary: "An antinomy exists when a pair of principles stand side by side, seemingly irreconcilable, yet both undeniable. There are cogent reasons for believing each of them: each rests on clear, solid evidence; but it is a mystery to you how they can be squared with each other. You see that each must be true on its own, but you do not see how they can both be true together."[6]

Packer goes on to add that modern physics faces an antinomy in its study of light, because there is strong evidence to show that light consists of waves and equally strong evidence to show that it consists of particles. It is not readily apparent how light can be both waves and particles, but cogent evidence is there, so neither view can be ruled out in favor of the other. He notes that "Neither, however, can be reduced to the other or explained in terms of the other; the two seemingly incompatible positions must be held together, and both must be treated as true. Such a necessity scandalizes our tidy minds, no doubt, but there is no help for it if we are to be loyal to the facts."[7]

The knowledge of a sovereign God and the freedom of a responsible people before Him are both clearly taught in Scripture. Therefore, despite our inability to harmonize the two truths, we must equally affirm both.

GOD'S KNOWLEDGE IS UNIVERSAL

God knows all persons, all things, all contingencies: "Nothing in all creation is hidden from God's sight. Everything is uncovered and laid bare before the eyes of Him to whom we must give account" (Heb 4:13). God's knowledge is absolutely comprehensive; not one single thing occurring anywhere escapes His knowledge.

Not only does God have complete knowledge of everything that transpires in nature and in human experience, but He also possesses full knowledge of all that happens in the supernatural realm: "If I ascend up into heaven, thou art there: if I make my bed in hell, behold, thou art there" (Ps 139:8 [KJV]). So even "hell is naked before Him, and destruction hath no covering" from our all-knowing God (Job 26:6 [KJV]). Without doubt, God's knowledge is all-inclusive.

GOD'S KNOWLEDGE IS INFINITE

The Bible makes it plain that God's knowledge is unlimited: Great is our Lord, and of great power: His understanding is infinite" (Ps 147:5 [KJV]). Just think, God not only knows all things, He also knows everything at once! That certainly contrasts with human knowledge. We humans fret to keep in mind some task we must do at a later time, but God has no such problem. He does not need to labor to recall anything, for He always knows all things without effort.

W.G.T. Shedd explains that God "neither remembers nor forgets, in the literal sense, because the whole of His knowledge is simultaneously and perpetually present."[8] Of course, when Scripture speaks of God "remembering" (Gen 8:1) or "forgetting" (Isa 49:15), it is simply using anthropomorphic language to convey spiritual truth just as it does when it refers to the eyes, hands, or feet of God.

The fact that God has unlimited knowledge is of great practical value to His people. It assures us that He knows what He is doing and that He can never be tricked or deceived. We can be confident, therefore, that those who falsely malign the reputation of others will not go unnoticed by God. They may fool those around them, but they can never fool the One whose knowledge is infinite.

GOD'S KNOWLEDGE IS INCOMPARABLE

Romans 11:33-36 refers to the uniqueness of God's knowledge with these words: "Oh, the depth of the riches of the wisdom and knowledge of God! How unsearchable are His judgments, and His paths beyond tracing out! Who has known the mind of the Lord? Or who has been His counselor? Who has ever given to God, that God should repay Him? For from Him and through Him and to Him are all things. To Him be the glory forever!"

The Psalmist also comments on the unlimited knowledge of God with these remarks: "How precious to me are your thoughts, O God! How vast is the sum of them!" (Ps 139:17); "Such knowledge is too wonderful for me, too lofty for me to attain" (Ps 139:6). How far exalted above the wisest woman or man is the knowledge of God! We know not what a day may bring, but all the future is open to His omniscient sight!

So, what does God know? He knows and judges all people, and every action taken, whether good or evil. God understands and knows about our past, present, and future difficulties and trials, as well as our joys and triumphs.

God, while not causing the wrongful use of free will by those who practice evil deeds, can with His foreknowledge prepare us for those things which will befall us in days and years to come. For example, we in America can look back now and see that God allowed President Bush to become our leader at this time in our history when strong leadership in war is so badly needed. Likewise, in other areas of our lives, God is cognizant of all contingencies and prepares us many times for the future in ways we do not recognize ahead of time.

Realizing that God knows all things should fill our hearts with praise and thanksgiving. The whole of our lives stand open to His gaze from the beginning. He foresees our every fall, our every sin; yet, praise be to God, He fixes his heart upon us and longs for our salvation. Oh, how the realization of this truth should bow us in wonder and praise and adoration before Him!

"Now unto the King eternal, immortal, invisible, the only wise God, be honor and glory for ever and ever" (1 Tim 1:17 [KJV]).

8

Does God Really Care?

America is definitely going through a very dark storm. Overseas, our country is waging an offensive war on terrorism, while here at home, it is also engaging in defensive strategy to prevent future terrorism. If that weren't enough, add to that the uncertainties of the stock market and the downturning of the economy with resultant industrial downsizing and layoff of workers. In addition, major American airlines, hotels, restaurants, and tourist attractions are struggling to stay solvent. To top that all off, fear and anxiety pervade as men and women contemplate the possibility of future events such as bio or chemical terrorism.

We are a people in crisis. In the midst of our troubling times, we struggle with questions, such as: Does God realize the difficulties we are facing? Is He going to do anything about our problems? Does He really care?

God's character certainly matters! In fact, what God is like is the single most important thing we can discover about Him. But how are we to find answers concerning God's character? I believe the Bible teaches that God really cares about all that happens in our lives. He is a merciful and loving God who understands our limitations, our weaknesses, and our temptations. His strength and love are available to sustain us in darkness and suffering, to comfort us in sorrow and grief, to encourage us in all situations and happenings of life. God's love is continually set forth in Scripture not only as a fact, but also as a blessing available to all who will trust in Him. No other quality of God's nature is so precious to the human soul than that of God's love.

One of the great passages on God's love and ours is 1 John 4:7-10: "Dear friends, let us love one another, for love comes from God. Everyone who loves has been born of God and knows God. Whoever does not love does not know God, because God is love. This is how God showed His love among us: He sent His one and only Son into the world that we might live through Him. This is love; not that we loved God, but that He loved us and sent His Son as an atoning sacrifice for our sins." God not only said He loved us, but also proved it by what Christ did.

However, the phrase from Scripture "God is love" does not give us the full outlook concerning that attribute. The Bible reveals that God is a being who exhibits a broad range of character traits associated with His love, such as the following: (1) God's love is holy and righteous; (2) God's love is merciful and patient; (3) God's love is faithful and unchanging; and (4) God's love is good and benevolent. A study of *all* these attributes as set forth in Scripture will help us to see that our Lord really does care.

God's Love Is Holy and Righteous

In the scriptural revelation of the character of God, the love of God and the holiness of God are held closely together. For example, in the Old Testament, God's love and holiness are linked in passages similar to the following: "The Lord is slow to anger, abounding in love and forgiving sin and rebellion. Yet He does not leave the guilty unpunished" (Num 14:18). Likewise, in the New Testament, God's love and holiness are connected in passages such as: "God demonstrates His own love for us in this: While we were still sinners, Christ died for us. Since we have now been justified by His blood, how much more shall we be saved from God's wrath through Him!" (Rom 5:8-9).

Numbers 14:18, Romans 5:8-9, and other Scriptures reveal that God in His essence is both love and holiness. Therefore, any sentimental ideas we may hold about God's love as an indulgent softness, divorced from moral standards, must be ruled out from the beginning. J.I. Packer stresses that God's love is holy love: "The God whom Jesus made known is not a God who is indifferent to moral distinction, but a God who loves righteousness and hates inequity."[1]

God has given to mankind a free will to do what we want, to make our own choices. And each of us will most certainly be held accountable for what we do. So we must not make the common mistake of thinking that because God is love that no one will be punished for his or her sins. Billy Graham points out that "God's holiness demands that all sin be punished, but God's love provides the plan and way of redemption for sinful man. God's love provided the cross of Jesus, by which man can have forgiveness and cleansing."[2]

Because God is holy, He cannot possibly ignore our sins. But because God is love, He can forgive them. He loves us so much that He has provided, at great cost to himself, an atonement for our sins. However, there is a condition. If we ignore the pardon offered us through Christ, God's holiness requires we pay the penalty for our own sin: "Whoever believes in Him is not condemned, but whoever does not believe stands condemned already because he has not believed in the name of God's one and only Son" (John 3:18). Nevertheless, God's wonderful provision of salvation proves with clarity the reality and the depth of His love.

Holiness is the essence of God's nature, but righteousness is that nature, or character, in action. Righteousness is that activity of God's holiness in which He always does what is just or right: "The Lord is righteous in all His ways and loving toward all He has made" (Ps 145:17).

William Evans writes that the righteousness and justice of God are revealed "in the punishment of the wicked (Psa. 11:4-7),…in forgiving the sins of the penitent (1 John 1:9),…in keeping His word and promise to His children (Neh. 9:7,8),…in showing Himself to be the vindicator of His people from all their enemies (Psa. 129:1-4),…[and] in the rewarding of the righteous (Heb. 6:10)."[3] The righteousness of God, then, guarantees that He will render to each man his due penalty or reward, as the case may be.

However, in view of the grim reality of future punishment for those who reject God's salvation, questions concerning God's righteousness present themselves to many folks in queries such as: What is the fate of those who have never heard? What is the fate of those who lived before Christ? What is the fate of those who are incapable of a response to the gospel?

THOSE WHO HAVE NEVER HEARD

Few questions have troubled the hearts and minds of people as greatly as the fate of those who have never heard. "Will a loving God eternally doom human beings who have never heard the message of the gospel?", they ask. "If so, how could we possibly commit ourselves to such a God?"

Concerning those who have never heard, it helps to remember that we do not know the scope of God's total activity in regard to them. C.S. Lewis, reflecting on this question, says that he used to be troubled by the thought that salvation "should be confined to people who have heard of Christ and been able to believe in Him. But the truth is God has not told us what His arrangements about the other people are. We do know that no man can be saved except through Christ; we do not know that only those who know Him can be saved through Him. But in the meantime, if you are worried about the people outside, the most unreasonable thing you can do is to remain outside yourself. Christians are Christ's body, the organism through which He works. Every addition to that body enables Him to do more."[4]

Although God has not revealed to us His plan for those who have never heard, we can count on Him to do the right thing in regard to these precious souls. In the meantime, we need to remember that God's normal pattern for reaching the lost remains the preaching of the gospel (Rom 10:15), because all people everywhere deserve a clearly understood invitation to the fullness of God's salvation. Hence, for the Christian there is a mandate to endeavor to spread the gospel.

Christ commissioned His followers to make disciples of all nations by baptizing and instructing them: "Therefore go and make disciples of all nations, baptizing them in the name of the Father and of the Son and of the Holy Spirit, and teaching them to obey everything I have commanded you. And surely I am with you always, to the very end of the age" (Matt. 28:19-20). Our

Lord's vision was of disciples making other disciples; we would do well to follow His commission.

THOSE WHO LIVED BEFORE CHRIST

Sometimes folks are concerned about those who lived before Christ, questioning how they could have come to a true knowledge of God. It must be remembered that the basis of salvation has always been the sacrificial death, burial, and resurrection of Jesus Christ.

Kenneth Boa and Larry Moody elaborate: "Though the saving work of Christ was future, God saw it from before the foundation of the earth. Not bound by time, the Lord applied the benefits of the death of Christ to all who called upon God for salvation. The means of salvation has always been faith, not works. The Old Testament clearly teaches that man is sinful and in need of God's grace (Isa. 59:2; 64:6; Ps. 6:1-2; 51:1-13). Thus, an Israelite needed to acknowledge his sin and turn to God in repentance and faith. The blood of the animal sacrifices did not save, but pointed ahead to the sacrifice of God's son. In Old Testament times, people did not clearly understand this; like Abraham (Gen 15:6), they were justified by grace through faith, and the object of that faith was God. But with the progressive revelation of the New Testament, the content of faith now includes the finished work of Christ."[5]

In all ages the basis of salvation has been the redemptive work of Christ and the means of salvation has always been grace through faith.

THOSE INCAPABLE OF A RESPONSE

Another problem some men and women struggle with concerns those mentally incapable of understanding the gospel—children and the severely retarded. What is their destiny?

What does the Bible say about the fate of children and the retarded? As we examine both the Old Testament and the New, we discover that the Scriptures are strangely silent on this subject. Barry Wood comments that "neither Jesus nor the apostles give us direct discourse on the status of children. Jesus said, 'Permit the children to come to me, and do not hinder them, for the kingdom of heaven belongs to such as these' (see Matthew 19:14). Again He said, 'Unless you are converted and become like children, you shall not enter the kingdom of heaven' (Matthew 18:3). These statements are about the only clues we have as to the status of children before God. Yet the silence of Scripture strongly testifies that children are 'innocent until proven guilty' as far as God is concerned."[6] It should be added that another instance in regard to children concerns King David, who, after the loss of his child, said, "Now that he is dead, why should I fast? Can I bring him back again? I will go to him, but he will not return to me" (2 Sam 12:22).

What are we to conclude then? Wood stresses that children below the age of responsibility and the mentally incompetent are kept under the special watchcare of Jesus: "Children are innocent until they individually respond to God in rebellion. This statement would imply that children or the mentally retarded are not accountable. Only God knows when a person is ready for the gospel. Some retarded persons never come to the age of accountability and are under God's watchcare, just like a little child. It is my understanding that children who die go immediately to be with the Lord, perhaps escorted by guardian angels (see Matthew 18:10) into the presence of God."[7]

Menno Simons concurs: "If they [children] die before coming to years of discretion, that is, in childhood, before they have come to years of understanding and before they have faith, then they die under the promise of God, that by no other means than the generous promise of grace through Christ Jesus. Luke 18:16."[8] For those who die previous to an age of understanding, God's love in Jesus Christ is completely effective.

Concerning the fate of those who have never heard, of those who lived before Christ, and of those who are incapable of a response to the gospel, we can trust the Judge of all the earth to assuredly do what is right (Gen 18:25). For the Lord "is righteous; He does no wrong. Morning by morning He dispenses His justice" (Zeph 3:5).

Because God is holy and righteous, we have foremost evidence that He truly cares. Only a holy and just God could demonstrate His love by sending His Son, Jesus Christ, into the world to die for our sins.

GOD'S LOVE IS MERCIFUL AND PATIENT

God's mercy is the divine love exhibited toward His creatures, feeling for their sufferings and making provision for their relief, and in the case of all sinners, leading to long-suffering patience.

God's love is revealed in His mercy and compassion in relation to all people, for "he causes His sun to rise on the evil and the good, and sends rain on the righteous and the unrighteous" (Matt 5:45). God pours out His mercy even on those who are in rebellion against Him, because "while we were still sinners, Christ died for us" (Rom 5:8). But God especially delights to show His mercy "to those who love me and keep my commandments" (Deut 5:10).

One of the most beautiful descriptions of God's mercy is Psalm 103:8-14: "The Lord is compassionate and gracious, slow to anger, abounding in love. He will not always accuse, nor will He harbor his anger forever; He does not treat us as our sins deserve or repay us according to our iniquities. For as high as the heavens are above the earth, so great is His love for those who fear Him; as far as the east is from the west, so far has He removed our transgressions from us. As a father has compassion on his children, so the Lord has compassion on those who fear Him; for He knows how we are formed, He remembers that we are dust."

God's love is also displayed in his patience expressed toward those who are properly and justly due His anger. Thank the Lord that He is a patient God who holds back from us what we deserve! For He is patient both with believers, forgiving unfaithfulness and sin, and with unbelievers, giving time to repent: "The Lord is not slow in keeping His promise, as some understand slowness. He is patient with you, not wanting anyone to perish, but everyone to come to repentance" (2 Pet 3:9).

Here is infinite patience manifested in God's loving forbearance with sinners. God doesn't demand or harangue us if we don't respond to His overtures. Instead, He continues to draw us by the force of His compelling love. Now that is Patience!

Let us beware, however, lest we "show contempt for the riches of His kindness, tolerance, and patience, not realizing that God's kindness leads you toward repentance…[because] for those who are self-seeking and who reject the truth and follow evil, there will be wrath and anger" (Rom 2:4, 8). Anger is not the basic disposition of God toward people, since He is "slow to anger." Yet it connotes the searing reaction of God to continued and willful disobedience of Him.

So another important way we can answer the question "Does God really care?" is by discovering the riches of His mercy and patience. For mercy is God's love understanding our limitations, weaknesses, and sins; and patience is His love displaying forbearance because it holds back from us what we really deserve. Both are demonstrations that God truly cares.

GOD'S LOVE IS FAITHFUL AND UNCHANGING

God is absolutely trustworthy and dependable. His love never fails! Whereas human love can fail, God's love is dependable 100 percent of the time. Speaking of God's love, Jeremiah writes: "The Lord appeared to us in the past, saying: 'I have loved you with an everlasting love; I have drawn you with loving-kindness'" (Jer 31:3). The God who loved and cared about Israel generations ago is exactly the same God who loves and cares for us today. You can count on it!

The depth of God's faithful love is rooted in the immutability of His character. The Bible teaches that God is the one with whom there "is no variableness, neither shadow of turning" (James 1:17 [KJV]). God is immutable, therefore, in the sense that His character or nature cannot change.

Some people question God's immutability, however, citing Scripture passages which state that God changed His mind in some way, concerning such instances as: making Saul king of Israel (1 Sam 15:11); judgments by locusts and fire (Amos 7:3,6); calamity if a nation should turn from evil (Jer 18:8); imminent punishment of Ninevites (Jonah 3:9) and so forth. "Do not these texts," they ask, "make it impossible to conclude that God is changeless?"

No! These passages rather bear out that God changes His behavior in accordance with the changes in human beings. Therefore, it is not His character that changes, but His response to a changing situation. His unchanging holiness requires Him to treat the disobedient differently from the obedient. But God's fundamental character and His overall purpose abide without alteration or deviation.

As Emil Brunner points out, the immutability of God's character does not exclude Him from interacting with His creation in an interpersonal way: "If it be true that there really is such a fact as the Mercy of God and the Wrath of God, then God, too, is 'affected' by what happens to His creatures. He is not like that divinity of Platonism who is unconcerned, and therefore unmoved, by all that happens upon the earth, but goes his way in heaven without looking round, without taking into consideration what is happening on earth. God does 'look round'—He does care what happens to men and women—He is concerned about the changes upon earth....God's behavior alters according to the behavior of man. For this very reason He is the living God, in contrast to the divinity of abstract thought."[9]

The Christian God is religiously available precisely because he is a personal, living God who interacts with His creatures. Indeed the change that accompanies God's interpersonal relations with His creatures is not a sign of imperfection, but of perfection. A personal God would lack perfection if He were incapable of relations with those He loved.

The fact remains that God in the essence of His character and purposes *never* changes. A God who changes in His nature would not be a God whom we could worship. But the God of the Bible is eternally faithful and unchangeable, the same from everlasting to everlasting. Thus we are shown once again that He is a God who faithfully loves and cares for His children.

GOD'S LOVE IS GOOD AND BENEVOLENT

The Bible proclaims time and again that the basic moral character of God is good and loving. His goodness is described as great (Ps 31:19), enduring (Ps 52:1), satisfying (Ps 65:4), and universal (Ps 145:9). It is the goodness of God that elicits both worship and obedience. God's glory may rightly bring awe and praise from His people, and God's holiness may evoke our perception of transgression and sin. But it is God's goodness that truly calls forth our reverence and compliance to His will.

God's benevolence is closely related to His goodness. As we understand good to refer to God's moral character, we understand benevolence to refer to His blessings bestowed upon mankind. In Scripture God's benevolence is manifested in material blessings (Acts 14:17), in spiritual blessings (Ps 31:19), and in the forgiveness of sin (Ps 86:5).

Scripture tells us that "God is light; in Him there is no darkness at all" (1 John 1:5). He is the absolute standard of goodness and benevolence. To some people, however, the existence of evil and suffering presents an obstacle to belief in the goodness and benevolence of God. "If God is so good," they ask, "why doesn't He do something about all the misery and pain in the world? Doesn't he understand? Doesn't he care?"

The Word of God teaches that the solution to these questions begins with the fact that God created mankind with genuine free will. Human beings, therefore, in freely choosing to sin and rebel against their Creator, deserve the blame for most of the resultant evil in our world. As Edward J. Carnell notes: "God is the author of the author of sin, but He cannot be the author of sin itself, for sin is the result of a rebellion against God. Can God rebel against Himself?"[10]

God created mankind free of sin, but He gave humanity the choice to love or to reject Him (Gen 1). The Bible says, therefore, that although God desires loving fellowship with human beings (2 Chr 16:9; Jer 29:11; John 4:23; 1 Peter 3:18), He did not force His love but gave people the privilege of free choice. He did this because He wanted freely reciprocated love from those He created, not the automatic love of spiritual robots or machines. In Genesis 2, God explained that mankind's obedience would bring continued fellowship and blessings, but mankind's disobedience would bring separation from His fellowship and physical death. Nevertheless, Genesis 3 tells us that mankind chose to disobey God rather than to obey Him. Humanity thus suffered the consequences of spiritual and physical death. Sadly, it was at this point the fall of mankind occurred and evil and suffering entered our world.

So we can see that God did not create nor is He responsible for evil and suffering. The plan of God had the potential for sin when He gave people freedom of choice, but the actual origin of evil came as a result of human free will. Within the limits of nature and social environment, mankind has freedom to choose good or evil; therefore, the greater part of human misery and pain is caused by mankind's propensity to sin.

On this subject, C.S. Lewis has written: "When souls become wicked they will certainly use this possibility to hurt one another; and this, perhaps, accounts for four-fifths of the sufferings of men. It is men, not

God, who have produced racks, whips, prisons, slavery, guns, bayonets, and bombs; it is by human avarice or human stupidity, not by the churlishness of nature, that we have poverty and overwork."[11]

In short, mankind's sin is the chief cause of the evil and suffering in our world. God does not cause terrorism, avarice, murder, jealousy, hate, and so forth. And, God does not heartlessly or thoughtlessly inflict suffering or misfortune on any of us. The God we know could not possibly do such a thing, "for He does not willingly bring affliction or grief to the children of men" (Lam 3:33).

The world is not as God intends it to be. He is going to make it right—but first He wants to change as many of us as are willing to fit into that perfect, sinless place. If He took us there the way we are now, we would mess that up too. He has chosen to not yet remove the cause of brokenness (us and our sin), nor the consequences of brokenness (suffering, pain, and death)—the first because He wants to save us, the second because of His holiness and His desire to help us know our need for salvation.

It is easy to associate moral evil with the fall of mankind. We can understand that such evil originates with human beings, rather than with God. Yet there remains much suffering which cannot be traced to the wrong choices of people. "What about natural evil?" some folks ask. "Are natural phenomena such as hurricanes, earthquakes, floods, and disease, which cause so much suffering and pain, mankind's fault?"

The key to understanding natural evil is provided by the fact that God works through orderly natural processes. Science has discovered and formulated many of these processes as "natural laws." These regularities are a great blessing to us, for we depend on them for our security in daily life. Nature *per se* is basically good, therefore, because it acts in accordance with God's established laws.

But, as William A. Spurrier relates: "Some of the effects of natural events *accidentally* harm humans and in that sense only is it evil. As to why this person and not that person gets hurt,...why this child gets this incurable disease and not that one, we do not know. This is the accidental and mysterious part of natural evil. We do not know. And we *emphatically* reject the answer which says that such accidents are punishment for sin. It is preposterous to say that a baby born a Mongoloid idiot must have sinned in his mother's womb and is thereby doomed to such a terrible if brief existence. And it is equally unjust to say that God is punishing the parents by taking it out on the child. Christianity does not believe in that kind of God."[12]

The God of Christianity is aware of the sufferings and needs of humanity and in His love he has done something about them. Though mankind brought death through rebellion, Christ came to earth to give life, not willing to let sin and suffering have the last word. Calvary's cross, then, is historical evidence that Christ Himself is involved in our pain: "He was despised and rejected by men, a man of sorrows, and familiar with suffering. Like one from whom men hide their faces He was despised, and we esteemed Him not. Surely He took up our infirmities and carried our sorrows, yet we considered Him stricken by God, smitten by Him, and afflicted. But He was pierced for our transgression, He was crushed for our iniquities; the punishment that brought us peace was upon Him, and by His wounds we are healed" (Isa 53:3-5).

Christ suffered greatly, "the just for the unjust, that He might bring us to God, being put to death in the flesh, but quickened by the Spirit" (1 Pet 3:18 [KJV]). He did this by entering into our little world, by becoming one of us, by finding out firsthand what it means to be ridiculed, to be lied about, to be misunderstood, to be mistreated, to be murdered.

So does God really care? The cross of Jesus Christ settled that question forever. The cross that held Christ's body, naked and marked with wounds, exposed all the violence and suffering and sin of this world. At once, the cross revealed the nature of our world and the nature of our God: a world of gross unfairness and pain; a God of eternal sacrifice and love.

9

Discover the Good

*W*hen we are shattered by tragic events, often we are so wounded that it seems incomprehensible that life could ever get back to a degree of normalcy. Emotional trauma can blind us to the possibility that the future holds any degree of healing and peace.

After my daughter Karen's death in 1982, I lived for some time in a perpetual state of depression and grief. Yet, with God's blessing and guidance, I have risen out of the mire of personal despair, by determining to assist others who are also seeking help in the aftermath of personal crisis or tragedy. If you were to ask me how I managed to bounce back, I would have to refer you to Romans 8:28: "And we know that in all things God works for the good of those who love Him, who have been called according to His purposes."

My own response to tragedy in life has been to look for the good that can come from the grief and the despair. Some might retort, however, that they can see no good that could possibly come out of anything as horrific as the calamity that has befallen America. Yet we must look. And, as we wipe our tearful eyes and peer beyond the devastation and the pain, we do see that in all things God does work for good.

What do we find? The first good thing we discover is a greater sense of harmony among the people of America. Differences in skin color, nationality, gender, or class do not seem to matter any more. And, we see a new tenderness and compassion demonstrated toward others even by those who previously displayed for the world an exterior shell of hardness and indifference.

Another good thing we find is that after the tragedy people have become more important than profit. The generous hearts of Americans have opened in an unprecedented way as donations have flooded relief agencies. This generous spirit says something dramatic and positive about the moral integrity of the American people.

The third thing we see is a renewed reverence and respect for human life that for many years had been absent in our culture. For example, in the wake of the attacks, every major sporting event in our nation was canceled for an entire week in a unprecedented demonstration of reverence and respect for those who lost their lives in New York, Washington, D.C., and Pennsylvania. In our sports loving nation, this action is something most of us never would have expected to see. In addition, many people in our country stayed home from work or from other activities, one or more days, out of respect for those who lost their lives, an attitude that bespeaks a great reverence for human life.

A fourth good thing we notice is that America's sense of invincibility disappeared when the suicidal terrorists brought down the World Trade Center towers and fractured a section of the Pentagon. Why is that good? Suddenly there is a general comprehension among the people that, ultimately, only God can protect and preserve the United States. Although we may eventually capture or kill most or even all of those responsible for the vicious attacks, nevertheless we know there are thousands of others ready and eager to take their place.

All our weapons, armament, financial resources, and political expertise are not enough to guarantee our protection. Only God can protect our nation. That is why it is so important that we turn our hearts back to God. As we plunge into the twenty-first century, with its unforeseen challenges and the prospect of even darker days ahead, we have nowhere else to turn but to God

A new spirit of patriotism is another good thing flowing from the calamity that has befallen us. Only a few years ago, some Americans were disrespectfully burning the American flag. But now, what a change of heart we see, as American patriots from sea to sea bear our national flag with utmost dignity and respect. Another aspect of the renewed spirit of patriotism is a sense of deep appreciation for all the brave soldiers who have gone before us and for those who so ably serve our country now.

A revived sense of things eternal is an additional good that has resulted from the crisis—we have become more interested in the spiritual rather than in the material or temporal aspects of our lives. Tragedy has forced us to face the difficult issues of suffering and death and eternal destiny. Thus we have an opportunity for introspection, not only into the quality of our lives, the legacies we will leave behind, but also into the futures we face for eternity. We reflect upon what kind of parents or grandparents we have been. One of my life's concerns relates to the legacy I will leave my grandsons Neal, Hunter, and Landon. What have I taught them concerning life's priorities? As I have sought to live life with integrity, have the positive aspects of my life outweighed the negative? These questions and many more are contemplated as I ponder eternity and how prepared I am to face my Father in heaven.

Perhaps you have also been reflecting on the legacy you will leave your loved ones and on your relationship with God. This is a natural reaction, because God so designed us that we experience a longing to draw near to him. Without a relationship with our Creator, we feel an inner emptiness, a hunger for fulfillment. The ultimate hunger, then, is for His love, an idea caught so well in Augustine's famous saying: "Our hearts are restless until they rest in thee."

Throughout this book we have honestly examined teachings about God as presented in the Bible. We have also examined the wonderful promises of God in regard to salvation and eternal life. Perhaps as you have read this book, you have realized that you have never experienced the security and peace that come from a personal relationship with Him.

If so, the invitation comes now for you to experience God for yourself, to "taste and see that the Lord is good" (Ps 34:8). For only an act of commitment which puts religion to the test, only this will satisfy your spiritual hunger for God.

But how, in practice, do you accept Christ personally and make a decision to follow Him? Scripture says, "Yet to all who received Him, to those who believed in His name, He gave the right to become children of God" (John 1:12). The verse tells us we are to "believe" and to "receive" Christ—we are to *believe* that He died on the cross for our sins and rose again from the dead so we might be saved, and we are to *receive* Him personally into our hearts by faith. For additional information on the means and the nature of our salvation, please check Appendix B.

If you haven't already done so, right now I invite you to pray a beautiful prayer people all over the world have prayed at Billy Graham Crusades, asking Christ to forgive them and inviting Him to come into their hearts as Lord and Savior. Will you sincerely pray the following prayer?

"Oh God, I know I am a sinner and need Your forgiveness. I believe that You died for my sins. I want to turn from my sins. I now invite You to come into my heart and life. I want to trust You as Savior and follow You as Lord, in the fellowship of Your church. In Christ's name, Amen."[1]

If you have accepted Christ into your heart and committed your life to Him, then God has forgiven you, adopted you into His family, and given you eternal life: "And this is the testimony; God has given us eternal life, and this life is in His Son" (1 John 5:11).

Becoming a Christian is your first step on the lifelong road of spiritual growth and of service to God. Follow Christ in believer's baptism as a public expression of your faith and join a local church. May God bless you as you commit your life to His Son and follow Him every day.

Truly, out of tragedy God can work all things together for triumph and good. Today, we have an opportunity, by faith, to believe in God and in each other for a better tomorrow, to share our resources and our love with those in need, and to rise above the tempest swirling around us as we give "thanks for all things in the name of our Lord" (Eph 5:20).

Appendix A

The following are some historical writings from non-Christian sources that testify to Jesus' existence and confirm the basic record of His life as recorded in the New Testament.

FLAVIUS JOSEPHUS

An early extrabiblical reference to Jesus is from the non-Christian Jewish historian, Flavius Josephus (A.D. 37-100). The clearest reference is quoted from an Arabic text of Josephus which antedates other known texts:[1] "At this time there was a wise man called Jesus, and his conduct was good, and he was known to be virtuous. And many people from among the Jews and other nations became his disciples. Pilate condemned him to be crucified and to die. And those who had become his disciples did not abandon their discipleship. They reported that he had appeared to them three days after his crucifixion and that he was alive. Accordingly, he was perhaps the Messiah concerning whom the prophets have recounted wonders."[2] Just think, a non-Christian wrote that!

PONTIUS PILATE

Procurator of Judea, Pontius Pilate, who condemned Christ to death, wrote of that event to Tiberius Caesar in a well-known account that has been referred to by several other historic personages. In the long report, after describing the miracles of Jesus, Pilate writes: "And him Herod and Archelaus and Philip, Annas and Caiaphas, with all the people, delivered to me, making a great uproar against me that I should try him [Christ]. I therefore ordered him to be crucified, having first scourged him, and having found against him no cause of evil accusations or deeds. And at the time he was crucified there was darkness over all the world, the sun being darkened at mid-day, and the stars appearing, but in them there appeared no lustre; and the moon, as if turned into blood, failed in her light."[3] Were you as surprised as I was to learn that quotes from Pontius Pilate actually existed?

THALLUS

The Gentile historian Thallus (c. A.D. 52), who wrote in the middle of the first century, tried to explain away the three-hour period of darkness at the time of Christ's crucifixion as a solar eclipse. Another writer Julius Africanus (A.D. 221), cites the writings of Thallus when he says: "Thallus, in the third book of his histories, explains away this darkness as an eclipse of the sun— unreasonable, as it seems to me."[4] A nonsupernatural explanation of the event isn't reasonable because Christ died at the time of Passover when there was a full moon, and a solar eclipse cannot take place at the time of a full moon.

MARA BAR-SERAPION

Another early reference to Jesus is a letter written during the first century (about A.D. 73) by a Syrian named Mara Bar-Serapion to his son. Warning the lad not to get involved in wicked deeds and reminding him of the terrible consequences that came upon people who killed godly men, he stated: "What advantage did the Jews gain from executing their wise King? It was just after that that their kingdom was abolished. God justly avenged these wise men...The Jews, ruined and driven from their land, live in complete dispersion."[5]

CORNELIUS TACITUS

An early second century reference to Jesus is from Cornelius Tacitus (born A.D. 52-54), a Roman historian who alludes to the death of Christ and to the existence of Christians at Rome during the reign of Caesar Nero. Tacitus records that Nero shifted the blame for the burning of Rome from himself to these early Christians: "Hence to suppress the rumor, he falsely charged with the guilt, and punished with the most exquisite tortures, the persons commonly called Christians, who were hated for their enormities. Christus, the founder of the name, was put to death by Pontius Pilate, procurator of Judea in the reign of Tiberius: but the pernicious super-stition, repressed for a time broke out again, not only through Judea, where the mischief originated, but through the city of Rome also" (*Annals*, XV. 44). Isn't it strange that this man was a non-Christian, yet his testi-mony helps validate the historical facts about Jesus?

PLINEY THE YOUNGER

Another second century reference is by Pliney the Younger (c. A.D. 112), the governor of Bithynia in Asia Minor, who sent an important document to the Emperor Trajan which clearly establishes, at a high official level, the historicity of Jesus. He had this to say about the

Christians: "They affirmed, however, that the whole of their guilt, or their error, was, that they were in the habit of meeting on a certain fixed day before it was light, when they sang in alternate verse a hymn to Christ as to a god, and bound themselves to a solemn oath, not to any wicked deeds, but never to commit any fraud, theft, adultery, never to falsify their word, not to deny a trust when they should be called upon to deliver it up" (*Epistles* X. 96).

SUETONIUS

An additional second century reference is from the Roman historian Suetonius (c. A.D. 120), who says: "As the Jews were making constant disturbances at the instigation of Chrestus (another spelling of Christus), he expelled them from Rome" (*Life of Claudius*, 25.4). This statement is particularly interesting in the light of Acts 18:2 where we read of a similar happening, this time from the Christian perspective.

LUCIAN OF SAMOSATA

Another writer, Lucian of Samosata (second century), a Greek satirist, spoke scornfully of Christ and the Christians. Connecting them with the synagogues of Palestine, he alluded to Christ as "the man who was crucified in Palestine because he introduced this new cult into the world....Furthermore, their first lawgiver persuaded them that they were all brothers one of another after they have transgressed once for all by denying the Greek gods and by worshipping that cruci-fied sophist himself and living under his laws" (*The Passing Peregrinus*).

THE TALMUD

A collection of Jewish writings, the Talmud, constituting the religious and civil laws and completed by A.D. 500, states: "On the eve of Passover they hanged Yeshu (of Nazareth)...[because] he hath practiced sorcery and beguiled and led astray Israel" (*Babylonia Sanhedrin* 43a, "Eve of Passover"). Another reference to Jesus in the Talmud, states: "R. Shimeon ben Azzai said [concerning Jesus]: 'I found a genealogical roll in Jerusalem wherein was recorded, Such-an-one is a bastard of an adulteress'" (*Yeb*, IV, 3.49a).

Did you notice that both Talmud references corroborate the New Testament picture of how unbelievers viewed Jesus? They accused him of being demon-possessed: "But when the Pharisees heard this, they said, 'It is only by Beelzebub, the prince of demons, that this fellow drives out demons'" (Matt 12:24). And they accused him of being illegitimate: "We are not illegitimate children" (John 8:41). The references to Jesus in the Talmud are clear evidence that Jesus was remembered among the Jews as a Rabbi who lived in the time before the fall of the temple.

Appendix B

The Bible makes it clear that faith is the means by which we receive the salvation purchased for us by Jesus Christ and enter into a relationship with God: "For it is by grace you have been saved, through faith—and this is not from yourselves, it is the gift of God—not by works, so that no one can boast" (Eph 2:8-9).

But what exactly is faith? Faith might be described as a total commitment of the whole person to the living Christ, a commitment that includes "the elements of knowledge (*notitia*),...intellectual assent (*assensus*),... and trust and venture (*fiducia*)."[1]

THE ELEMENT OF KNOWLEDGE

The first element of faith involves knowledge of the objective facts concerning Christianity. Faith entails such knowledge, for there must be objective truth for us to believe in: "Biblical faith is always bound up in knowledge. Without knowledge faith becomes crude and blind credulity. We have already seen that faith is not just belief, but biblical faith cannot exist without beliefs. The Bible does not regard faith as unintelligent action. That is why so much emphasis is placed upon proclamation. Men must hear the gospel before they can 'faith' the Lord. They need to know certain facts. Peter's sermon at Pentecost, found in Acts 2, is a good example of the New Testament stress upon knowing."[2] In this particular situation, on the day of Pentecost, Peter clearly proclaimed the objective truth of the gospel to many people in Jerusalem and 3,000 were saved (Acts 2:22-41).

121

So the Bible teaches that faith has a cognitive content, a rational quality. Our object of faith is both a living God, and a particular message about Him. The first element of faith, therefore, is knowledge of the objective facts of the Christian gospel.

THE ELEMENT OF INTELLECTUAL ASSENT

Acknowledging the objective facts of the Christian message is the second element of faith. We not only notice the facts to be believed, but also give assent to them in our minds. In other words, faith is *believing* on the basis of objective evidence.

It should be mentioned here that doubt presents a hindrance to faith for some people, for they feel they can't decide for Christ until *all* their doubts are removed. But to know God is not a matter of knowing all about Him. God is far beyond our limited knowledge and comprehension. Only the most arrogant person, therefore, would claim to know all about God. "Oh, the depth of the riches of the wisdom and knowledge of God! How unsearchable His judgments, and His paths beyond tracing out! Who has known the mind of the Lord? Or who has been His counselor?" (Rom 11:33-34).

Faith is not the absence of all doubt, it is a decision based on the evidence at hand. We have to live and act on the basis of the limited human knowledge we possess. Do we know enough to at least admit the possibility that God might exist and that the gospel might be true? If so, we can go on to take a venture of faith in spite of doubt, for "true Christianity calls us to one further action and that is to follow. Just as there can be no actual swimming until you take the plunge, there can be no actual believing in God until we are prepared to follow Christ"[3]

THE ELEMENT OF TRUST AND VENTURE

As noted, the elements of knowledge and intellectual assent are important, but alone they cannot make a person into a Christian. The Bible tells us that a faith that encompasses only intellectual belief is not enough, for even demons have this type of faith (James 2:19). Demons recognize the existence of God and all His works, but their belief makes no difference in their conduct.

Thus biblical faith involves not only intellectual belief but also personal trust and commitment to God. For salvation comes not just from knowing *about* God but from personally accepting his offer of salvation.

It is only after a person has taken the "plunge" that "he finds that his subjective experiences of God confirm to his heart the truth of Christianity. Both the objective evidence and his subjective experience now point to the existence of God. Moreover, as his relationship with God develops, God helps him to understand more of His truth. Thus understanding and knowledge of God increase."[4]

It is God Himself who opens the eyes and hearts of people to the truth about Himself: "In other words, knowledge of God as Father and Jesus Christ as Lord and Savior does not come by human discovery, but by divine revelation. As sinners separated from God we have no mind for His truth, until the moment comes suddenly or quietly, when we are left saying, 'I see it now.' This is the work of the Spirit. He opens our eyes and our hearts to the truth that we could not see for ourselves."[5]

We have observed that the means of salvation include knowledge of the gospel, intellectual assent to its truth, and trust and acceptance of its offer. Now we will turn to the nature of our salvation, which includes: (1) justification; (2) regeneration; and (3) sanctification.

JUSTIFICATION

What does the term *justification* mean? In brief, it means that our salvation is God's gift and not our own achievement. Salvation does not come by the law: "Therefore no one will be declared righteous in His sight by observing the law; rather, through the law we become conscious of sin" (Rom 3:20). Nor does salvation come by human works: "God,...has saved us and called us to a holy life—not because of anything we have done but because of His own purpose and grace" (2 Tim 1:8-9).

What God requires of us are repentance, faith, and the acceptance of His forgiveness and mercy. Salvation, therefore, is the free gift of God's grace who "demonstrates His own love for us in this: while we were still sinners, Christ died for us" (Rom 5:8).

Hence, justification does not mean that an individual is just or righteous but that he or she is declared just or righteous. It is the imputed righteousness of the guilty before God: "God made Him who had no sin to be sin for us, so that in Him we might become the righteousness of God." (2 Cor 5:21).

A common misunderstanding concerning justification concerns the relationship between faith and works. Does the fact that we are saved by faith and not by works mean that we should refrain from good works? Myer Pearlman provides an excellent answer to the question: "The following is Scriptural teaching concerning the relation between faith and works. Faith is opposed to works when by works we mean good deeds upon which a person depends for salvation (Gal 3:11). However, a living faith will produce works (James 2:26), just as a living tree will produce fruit. Faith is justified and approved by works (James 2:18), just as the soundness of the roots of a good fruit-tree is indicated by its fruit. Faith is perfected in works (James 2:22), just as a flower is completed by its blossom. In brief, works are the result of faith, the test of faith, and the consummation of faith."[6]

To sum up, justification is a judicial term whereby an individual, guilty and condemned before God, is acquitted and declared righteous or justified. The nature of justification is divine acquittal; the necessity for justification is mankind's condemnation; the source of justification is grace; the ground of justification is Christ's righteousness; and the means of justification is faith.

REGENERATION

What is meant by the word *regeneration*? The Bible provides a scriptural definition: "Therefore, if anyone is in Christ, he is a new creation; the old has gone, the new has come!" (2 Cor 5:17).

When someone becomes a Christian, that person is "born again" (John 3:3) as a brand new man or woman, with a new nature and approach to life affecting his or her behavior, thinking, and disposition. J. Dwight Pentecost elaborates on the nature of the new birth: "One who is born into this world spiritually dead must be born a second time, of a new Father, into a new family, if he is to have eternal life and is to become the child of God. Human beings, apart from Adam, came into this world only one way, by a process of birth. This is the result of conception where the parents gave to the child the nature, the life, which they themselves possessed. If we are to be born into God's family, it must be through a miracle of a new birth, of a new Father who can give a new nature to us, so that we may be called the sons or the children, of God"[7]

On becoming a Christian, a person enters into a vital union with God in Christ. He or she becomes a child of God, a new creation of God. Individuals who have entered this relationship truly "know" God in intimate fellowship.

Thus the new Christian has found what is most important in life. Nothing else is essential for joy and happiness—not fame, not fortune, not pleasure, not even health. Though earthly benefits can add to one's happiness in Christ, they cannot of themselves yield lasting contentment. What is most important is the joy that comes from being forgiven, from being reconciled to God through Christ, and from being in personal communion with him. For knowing God gives more fulfillment than anything else in the world. A relationship with God is not only the basis for a meaningful life here and now, but also the basis for our future immortality.

J.I. Packer expressed it so well: "What makes life worth while is having a big enough objective, something which catches our imagination and lays hold of our allegiance; and this the Christian has, in a way that no other man has. For what higher, more exalted, and more compelling goal can there be than to know God?"[8]

In summary, regeneration is the new life imparted by the Holy Spirit whereby a person becomes a child of God. The nature of regeneration is the new birth; the necessity of regeneration is mankind's need for transformation; and the means of regeneration is divine agency.

SANCTIFICATION

What is the meaning of the expression *sanctification*? The purpose of God in sanctification is the production of holy men and women set apart for the service of God. Herschel H. Hobbs notes that sanctification has a threefold nature: "It is instantaneous in that the moment we trust in Jesus we are dedicated to God and his service (Acts 9:6, 15-16)....It is continuous in that we go on growing in grace, and in the knowledge and service of our Lord and Savior Jesus Christ' (2 Peter 3:18)....Salvation is ultimate in that those who are genuinely saved will persevere in fruit bearing (Matt. 3:8; 7:16; John 15:2-16) unto the final perfection and reward which they will receive in heaven (John 4:36-37; cf. Matt. 25:14-46)."[9]

Two erroneous viewpoints of sanctification should be mentioned. One false view is that sanctification gives license for loose living. In other words, some may ask: Since we are justified not by law but by grace, why should we refrain from sinning? Why not continue in sin to obtain more grace?

The Bible points out that such an attitude is wrong: "What shall we say, then? Shall we go on sinning so that grace may increase? By no means! We died to sin; how can we live in it any longer? Or don't you know that all of us who were baptized into Christ Jesus were baptized into his death? We were therefore buried with him through baptism into death in order that, just as Christ was raised from the dead through the glory of the Father, we too may live a new life" (Rom 6:1-4). In other words, Jesus Christ died for sin in order that we might die to sin.

Although we are called to freedom in Christ instead of to slavery to law, we are not to use our "freedom to indulge the sinful nature; rather, [we are to] serve one another in love" (Gal 5:13). We are to bring our life into line with God's ethical standards, certainly not to earn salvation, but to prepare ourselves for proper service to God and others.

Another incorrect view is that sanctification refers to perfection. Scripture clearly teaches, however, that as long as we are in our earthly bodies we will have sin (Rom 7:14-25; James 3:2; 1 John 1:6-10). The Christian recognizes that no day is lived in practical righteousness or perfection. We stumble daily in large and small ways, and we stand convicted before a holy and righteous God. Even the best Christians must repeatedly ask for forgiveness when they lose moral battles.

In our battles against sin, though, we do not fight alone, for there is a "work of the Holy Spirit by which we are progressively being conformed in our daily experience to the Lord Jesus Christ [2 Cor 3:18]. We are being changed into the same image, going from glory to glory. Our position before God is that we are sanctified, set apart unto God; our experience is that we are being sanctified in daily life, by the Spirits power, as we grow in grace and in knowledge, and as we are controlled by the Spirit of God."[10]

Ultimately, at the coming of Christ, we will be translated out of this sphere of sin and into his glory, and we shall be like Him: "Dear friends, now we are children of God, and what we will be has not yet been made known. But we know that when He appears, we shall be like Him, for we shall see Him as He is" (1 John 3:2). Our sanctification will be complete, then, for our experience will conform to our position throughout the unending ages of eternity!

In short, sanctification means that a Christian, set right in relation to God and born again to a new life, is dedicated to the service of God. The nature of sanctification is consecration; the time of sanctification is instantaneous, continuous, and ultimate; and the means of sanctification is divine action.

Thus a saved person is someone who has been set right with God, adopted into the divine family, and dedicated to God's service. His or her experience of salvation consists of justification, regeneration, and sanctification. All three aspects constitute full salvation.

Notes

CHAPTER 1

[1]John Leland, Ginny Carroll, Peter Katel, Peter Annin, and Andrew Murr, "Why the Children?", *Newsweek* (May 1, 1995), p. 48.

[2]Elie Wiesel, *Night* (New York, NY: Avon Books, 1969), p. 9.

[3]Barbara Kantrowitz, Patricia King, Debra Rosenberg, Karen Springen, Pat Wingert, Tessa Namuth, and T. Trent Gegax, "In Search of the Sacred," *Newsweek* (November 28, 1994), p. 53.

CHAPTER 2

[1]George Carey, *Why I Believe in a Personal God* (Wheaton, IL: Harold Shaw Publishers, 1989), p. 28.

[2]Michael Green, *Faith for the Non-Religious* (Wheaton, IL: Tyndale House Publishers, 1979), p. 46.

[3]Ernest S. Williams, *Systematic Theology* (Springfield, MO: Gospel Publishing House, 1953), I, 169.

[4]Dallas M. Roark, *The Christian Faith* (Grand Rapids, MI: Baker Book House, 1969), pp. 7-8.

[5]As quoted by Myer Pearlman, *Knowing the Doctrines of the Bible* (Springfield, MO: Gospel Publishing House, 1990), p. 40.

[6]Clark H. Pinnock, *Set Forth Your Case* (Chicago, IL: Moody Press, 1971), p. 68.

[7]Godfrey C. Robinson and Stephen F. Winward, *Here Is the Answer* (Grand Rapids, MI: Zondervan, 1958), p. 24.

[8]J. Gilchrist Lawson, *Greatest Thoughts About Jesus Christ* (New York, NY: Richard R. Smith, Inc., 1919), p. 160.

[9]Michael Green, *Man Alive* (Downers Grove, IL: Inter-Varsity Press, 1968), p. 33.

[10]©1983 Cook Communications Ministries *Know Why You Believe* by Paul Little. Reprinted with permission. May not be further reproduced. All rights reserved.

[11]Ibid., p. 50.

[12]Josh McDowell, *Evidence That Demands a Verdict* (San Bernardino, CA: Here's Life Publishers, 1979), p. 225.

[13]John R.W. Stott, *Basic Christianity* (Downers Grove, IL: Inter-Varsity Press, 1971), p. 51.

[14]Pinnock, p. 99.

CHAPTER 3

[1]Billy Graham, *Peace with God* (Minneapolis, MN: Grason, 1984), p. 38.

[2]Alan Richardson, *The Gospel and Modern Thought* (London: Oxford University Press, 1950), p. 74.

[3]Barry Seagren, "Who Is God?", *What in the World Is Real?* (Champaign, IL: Communication Institute, 1982), pp. 299-300.

[4]Carey, p. 48.

[5]Joseph F. Green Jr., *Faith to Grow On* (Nashville, TN: Broadman Press, 1960), p. 46.

[6]D.A. Carson, "The Personal God," *Eerdmans' Handbook to Christian Belief* (Grand Rapids, MI: Wm. B. Eerdmans Publishing, 1982), p. 150.

[7]Frances J. Roberts, *Come Away, My Beloved* (Northridge, CA: Voice Publications, 1970), p. 81.

CHAPTER 4

[1]Taken from the exposition of Herschel H. Hobbs, *The Baptist Faith and Message* (Nashville, TN: Convention Press, 1971).

[2]R.A. Finlayson, "Trinity," *The New Bible Dictionary* (Grand Rapids, MI: Wm. B. Eerdmans Publishing, 1962), p. 1300.

[3]Kenneth Boa, *Unraveling the Big Questions About God* (Grand Rapids, MI: Lamplighter Books, 1988), pp. 43,45.

[4]Ibid., p. 45.

[5]Graham, p. 93.

[6]Josh McDowell and Don Stewart, *Answers to Tough Questions* (San Bernardino, CA: Here's Life Publishers, 1983), p. 72.

CHAPTER 5

[1]Philip Yancey, *Disappointment with God* (New York, NY: Harper Paperbacks, 1988), pp. 226-227.

[2]Boa, p. 141.

[3]David Field and Peter Toon, *Real Questions* (Belleville, MI: Lion Publishing Corporation, 1982), p. 80.

[4]Peter H. Gott, M.D., "An Out-of-This World Discovery," *The Clinton Daily Democrat* (February 21, 1996), p. 6.

CHAPTER 6

[1]See: Charles C. Ryrie, *A Survey of Bible Doctrine* (Chicago, IL: Moody Press, 1972), p. 22.

[2]Don Stewart, *103 Questions People Ask Most about God* (Wheaton, IL: Tyndale House Publishers, 1987), p. 55.

[3]William Rowe, *Philosophy of Religion* (Encino, CA: Dickenson, 1987), p. 9.

[4]Arthur W. Pink, *The Attributes of God* (Grand Rapids, MI: Baker Book House, 1975), p. 50.

CHAPTER 7

[1]Ibid., p. 17.

[2]John R. Rice, *Predestined for Hell! No!* (Murfreesboro, TN: Sword of the Lord Foundation, 1958), p. 91.

[3]Pat Robertson, *Answers to 200 of Life's Most Probing Questions* (Nashville, TN: Thomas Nelson Publishers, 1984), p. 58.

[4]A.W. Tozer, *The Divine Conquest* (Harrisburg, PA: Christian Publications, 1950), p. 21.

[5]Paul E. Little, *Know What You Believe* (Wheaton, IL: Victor Books, 1984), p. 42.

[6]J.I. Packer, *Evangelism and the Sovereignty of God* (Chicago, IL: Inter-Varsity Press, 1961), p. 18.

[7]Ibid., p. 19.

[8]W.G.T. Shedd, *Dogmatic Theology* (Grand Rapids, MI: Zondervan, n.d.), I, p. 384.

CHAPTER 8

[1]Taken from *Knowing God* by J. I. Packer. © 1973 J. I. Packer. Use by permission of InterVarsity Press, P.O. Box 1400, Downers Grove, IL 60515. www.ivpress.com

[2]Graham, p. 40.

[3]William Evans, *The Great Doctrines of the Bible* (Chicago, IL: Moody Press, 1980), pp. 42-43.

[4]C.S. Lewis, *Mere Christianity* (New York, NY: Macmillan Publishing, 1952), p. 65.

[5]Kenneth Boa and Larry Moody, *I'm Glad You Asked* (Wheaton, IL: Victor Books, 1982), p. 157.

[6]Barry Wood, *Questions Non-Christians Ask* (Old Tappan, NJ: Fleming H. Revell, 1977), p. 98.

[7]Ibid., p. 100.

[8]Menno Simons, "Christian Baptism," *The Complete Works of Menno Simons* (Scottdale, PA: Herald Press, 1956), p. 241.

[9]Emil Brunner, *The Christian Doctrine of God* (Philadelphia, PA: The Westminster Press) I, 268-269.

[10]Edward J. Carnell, *An Introduction to Christian Apologetics* (Grand Rapids, MI: Wm. B. Eerdman's Publishing, 1948), p. 302.

[11]C.S. Lewis, *The Problem of Pain* (New York, NY: Macmillan Publishing, 1962), p. 89.

[12]William A. Spurrier, *Guide to the Christian Faith* (New York, NY: Charles Scribner's Sons, 1952), p. 173.

CHAPTER 9

[1]Billy Graham, *Facing Death and the Life After* (Waco, TX: Work Books, 1987), p. 273.

APPENDIX A

[1]See: E.M. Blaiklock, *Jesus Christ: Man or Myth?* (Nashville, TN: Thomas Nelson Publishers, 1984), especially pp. 30-31.

[2]This passage is found in the Arabic manuscript "Kitab Al-Unwan Al-Mukallai Bi-Fadail Al-Hikma Al-Mutawwaj Bi-Anwa Al-Falsafa Al-Manduh Bi-Haqaq Al-Marifa" by Agapius, an Arab bishop of Baghdad.

[3]*The Ante-Nicene Fathers* (Grand Rapids, MI: William B. Eerdmans Publishing, 1951), VIII, 460-461.

[4]See: Josh McDowell, *Evidence That Demands a Verdict* (San Bernardino, CA: Here's Life Publishers, 1979), p. 84.

[5]Ibid., pp. 84-85.

APPENDIX B

[1]Donald G. Bloesch, *Essentials of Evangelical Theology* (San Francisco, CA: Harper and Row, 1978), I, 224.

[2]David K. Alexander and C.W. Junker (eds.), *What Can You Believe?* (Nashville, TN: Broadman Press, 1966), pp. 46-47.

[3]Carey, p. 139.

[4]Roger T. Forster and V. Paul Marston, *That's a Good Question* (Wheaton, IL: Tyndale House Publishers, 1971), p. 61.

[5]George Carey, "Finding Faith," *Eerdmans' Handbook to Christian Belief* (Grand Rapids, MI: Wm. B. Eerdmans Publishing, 1982), p. 358.

[6]Pearlman, p. 241.

[7]J. Dwight Pentecost, *Things Which Become Sound Doctrine* (Grand Rapids, MI: Zondervan, 1969), p. 31.

[8]Taken from *Knowing God* by J. I. Packer. ©1973 J. I. Packer. Used by permission of InterVarsity Press, P.O. Box 1400, Downers Grove, IL 60515. www.ivpress.com

[9]Hershel H. Hobbs, *Fundamentals of Our Faith* (Nashville, TN: Broadman Press, 1960), pp. 108-109.

[10]Pentecost, p. 119.

Works Cited

Alexander, David K. and C.W. Junker (eds.). *What Can You Believe?*. Nashville, TN: Broadman Press, 1966.

Blaiklock, E.M. *Jesus Christ: Man or Myth?*. Nash ville, TN: Thomas Nelson Publishers, 1984.

Bloesch, Donald G. *Essentials of Evangelical Theology.* San Francisco, CA: Harper and Row, 1978, I.

Boa, Kenneth. *Unraveling the Big Questions About God.* Grand Rapids, MI: Lamplighter Books, 1988.

Boa, Kenneth and Larry Moody. *I'm Glad You Asked?*. Wheaton, IL: Victor Books, 1982.

Brunner, Emil. *The Christian Doctrine of God.* Phila delphia, PA: The Westminster Press, I.

Carey, George. *Why I Believe in a Personal God.* Wheaton, IL: Harold Shaw Publishers, 1989.

_____. "Finding Faith," *Eerdmans' Handbook to Chris tian Belief.* Grand Rapids, MI: Wm. B. Eerdmans Publishing, 1982.

Carnell, Edward J. *An Introduction to Christian Apologetics.* Grand Rapids, MI: Wm. B. Eerdmans Publishing, 1948.

Carson, D.A. "The Personal God," *Eerdmans' Hand book to Christian Belief.* Grand Rapids, MI: Wm. B. Eerdmans Publishing, 1982.

Evans, William. *The Great Doctrines of the Bible.* Chicago, IL: Moody Press, 1980.

Field, David and Peter Toon. *Real Questions.* Belleville, MI: Lion Publishing Corporation, 1982.

Finlayson, R.A. "Trinity," *The New Bible Dictionary.* Grand Rapids, MI: Wm. B. Eerdmans Publishing, 1962, p. 1300.

Forster, Roger T. and V. Paul Marston. *That's a Good Question.* Wheaton, IL: Tyndale House Publishers, 1971.

Gott, Peter H. "An Out-of-This World Discovery," *The Clinton Daily Democrat*, February 21, 1996.

Graham, Billy. *Peace with God.* Minneapolis, MN: Grason, 1984.

Graham, Billy. *Facing Death and the Life After.* Waco, TX: Word Books, 1987

Green, Joseph F., Jr. *Faith to Grow On.* Nashville, TN: Broadman Press, 1960.

Green, Michael. *Faith for the Non-Religious.* Wheaton, IL: Tyndale House Publishers, 1979.

_____. *Man Alive*. Downers Grove, IL: Inter-Varsity Press, 1968.

Hobbs, Herschel H. *Fundamentals of Our Faith*. Nashville, TN: Broadman Press, 1960.

_____. *The Baptist Faith and Message*. Nashville, TN: Convention Press, 1971.

Kantrowitz, Barbara, Patricia King, Debra Rosenberg, Karen Springen, Pat Wingert, Tessa Namuth, and T. Trent Gegax. "In Search of the Sacred," *Newsweek*, November 28, 1994.

Lawson, J. Gilchrist. *Greatest Thoughts About Jesus Christ*. New York, NY: Richard R. Smith, Inc., 1919.

Leland, John, Ginny Carroll, Peter Katel, Peter Annin, and Andrew Murr. "Why the Children," *Newsweek*, May 1, 1995.

Lewis, C.S. *Mere Christianity*. New York, NY: Macmillan Publishing, 1952.

_____. *The Problem of Pain*. New York, NY: Macmillan Publishing, 1962.

Little, Paul E. *Know Why You Believe*. Wheaton, IL: Victor Books, 1983.

_____. *Know What You Believe*. Wheaton, IL: Victor Books, 1984.

McDowell, Josh. *Evidence That Demands a Verdict.* San Bernardino, CA: Here's Life Publishers, 1979.

McDowell, Josh and Don Stewart. *Answers to Tough Questions.* San Bernardino, CA: Here's Life Publishers, 1983.

Packer, J.I. *Evangelism and the Sovereignty of God.* Chicago, IL: Inter-Varsity Press, 1961.

_____. *Knowing God.* Downers Grove, IL: Inter-Varsity Press, 1973.

Pearlman, Myer. *Knowing the Doctrines of the Bible.* Springfield, MO: Gospel Publishing House, 1990.

Pentecost, Dwight J. *Things Which Become Sound Doctrine.* Grand Rapids, MI: Zondervan, 1969.

Pink, Arthur W. *The Attributes of God.* Grand Rapids, MI: Baker Book House, 1975.

Pinnock, Clark H. *Set Forth Your Case.* Chicago, IL: Moody Press, 1971.

Rice, John R. *Predestined for Hell! No!.* Murfreesboro, TN: Sword of the Lord Foundation, 1958.

Richardson, Alan. *The Gospel and Modern Thought.* London: Oxford University Press, 1950.

Roark, Dallas M. *The Christian Faith.* Grand Rapids, MI: Baker Book House, 1969.

Roberts, Frances J. *Come Away, My Beloved.* Northridge, CA: Voice Publications, 1970.

Robertson, Pat. *Answers to 200 of Life's Most Probing Questions.* Nashville, TN: Thomas Nelson Publishers, 1984.

Robinson, Godfrey C. and Stephen F. Winward. *Here Is the Answer.* Grand Rapids, MI: Zondervan, 1958.

Rowe, William. *Philosophy of Religion.* Encino, CA: Dickenson, 1987.

Ryrie, Charles C. *A Survey of Bible Doctrine.* Chicago, IL: Moody Press, 1972.

Seagren, Barry. "Who Is God?", *What in the World Is Real?.* Champaign, IL: Communications Institute, 1982.

Shedd, W.G.T. *Dogmatic Theology.* Grand Rapids, MI: Zondervan, n.d., I.

Simons, Menno. "Christian Baptism," *The Complete Works of Menno Simons.* Scottsdale, PA: Herald Press, 1956.

Spurrier, William A. *Guide to the Christian Faith.* New York, NY: Charles Scribner's Sons, 1952.

Stewart, Don. *103 Questions People Ask Most About God.* Wheaton, IL: Tyndale House Publishers, 1987.

Stott, John R.W. *Basic Christianity*. Downers Grove, IL: Inter-Varsity Press, 1971.

The Anti-Nicene Fathers. Grand Rapids, MI: William B. Eerdmans Publishing, 1951, VIII.

Tozer, A.W. *The Divine Conquest*. Harrisburg, PA: Christian Publications, 1950.

Wiesel, Elie. *Night*. New York, NY: Avon Books, 1969.

Williams, Ernest S. *Systematic Theology*. Springfield, MO: Gospel Publishing House, 1953.

Wood, Barry. *Questions Non-Christians Ask*. Old Tappan, NJ: Fleming H. Revell, 1977.

Yancey, Philip. *Disappointment with God*. New York, NY: Harper Paperbacks, 1988

To Order More Copies of This Book
Mail Check for $17.49
(includes priority mail shipping)
Sales Tax: Add 5.225% for shipping to MO addresses
To:
DOGWOOD PUBLISHING
116 WEST BUFFALO
BOLIVAR, MO 65613

Name _____

Address _____

City _____State_____Zip _____

Telephone _____

email address _____

Printed in the United States
6110